FAMILY CRESTS OF JAPAN

FAMILY CRESTS OF JAPAN

Stone Bridge Press • Berkeley, California

ACKNOWLEDGMENTS

The publisher gratefully thanks Takamori Ikuya for his translation, and acknowledges Jeff Huffman for his contribution to this book.

Published by
Stone Bridge Press, P.O. Box 8208, Berkeley, California 94707
tel 510-524-8732 • sbp@stonebridge.com • www.stonebridge.com

Originally published in 2001 by ICG Muse, Inc.

Revised edition © 2007 Stone Bridge Press.

Printed in the United States of America.

2011   2010   2009   2008   2007   10   9   8   7   6   5   4   3   2   1

ISBN 978-1-933330-30-3

CONTENTS

INTRODUCTION

Japanese family crests, or *kamon*, are traditional designs used to symbolize family names. Although there are various theories about their exact origin, it is generally accepted that kamon started as patterns on the palanquins, oxcarts, and garments of court nobles around the twelfth century. Gradually, use of the crests spread to the warrior class, and later to the common classes.

The motifs for many of the crests were plants, probably because the Japanese have admired and respected nature since ancient times. Unlike the highly colorful family crests of Europe, Japanese kamon are black and white, and most of the designs are two-dimensional and symmetrical.

Initially, the images of some kamon were more true to life and colorful. But when it became common practice for families to place kamon on clothing as a form of identification, kamon designs developed gradually into the style seen today. Although they are monochrome, kamon make the best artistic use of sharp black-and-white contrast, straight and curved lines, sharp angles, and simple geometric shapes. As a result, the traditional symbols achieve a surprisingly fresh, clear, sophisticated, and aesthetically pleasing style. Furthermore, kamon designs depict Japanese life, thought, and even history, making them valuable cultural assets as well as works of art.

Outside of Japan, crests were used only in Europe, where they seem to have originated around the twelfth century. In those days, Europe was fraught with wars between feudal lords and kingdoms. The style at the time was for European warriors to wear helmets that covered their heads entirely. These protective yet confining helmets narrowed the wearer's field of vision, and as a result, the custom of drawing symbols on shields to identify allies and enemies developed. These symbols were the source of the European crest, called a "coat of arms."

European knights often depicted animals as motifs on their crests, probably because Europe had a long cultural tradition of hunting and stock farming. Today, European coats of arms are still used on buildings, labels, stamps, and other prominent items. Though the crests of Europe and those of Japan contrast greatly in color, style, and motifs, it is interesting to note that both originated at about the same time in history.

In Japan, crests were regarded as an important symbol of a household, so by tradition, they were closely related with families. After World War II, however, as the definition of family changed, so did the meaning of the family crest. Modernization caused a rapid trend toward the nuclear family, resulting in the emergence of new, untraditional lifestyles, as well as increased societal emphasis on the individual and less on the family. Therefore, crests gradually lost their significance in society, and it was feared that their usage might die out.

Despite all this, kamon still prevail today and seem to have established a permanent place in Japanese society. They can be seen in modern Japan, especially at ceremonial events. Men wear kimono such as *montsuki haori hakama* (kimono jackets with family crests and full, flowing, pleated trousers), and women often wear *tomesode* (regular-sleeve-length kimono with patterns and family crests). These formal kimono, worn especially at traditional Japanese-style weddings, are in the seemingly sober colors of black and white; nevertheless, their refined and quiet elegance rivals the beauty of bright colors and showy patterns.

During wakes, mourners light lanterns marked with their kamon, brightly illuminating the dark night. The scene always impresses visitors with the strong, continued sense of "the family" and encourages visiting relatives to reaffirm their family ties. In graveyards, family crests appear in a wide variety of designs and motifs. Most of them are engraved on tombstones, distinguishing the burial sites of different families.

Kamon are not only found at weddings and funerals. You can still find crests in many places as you walk along the streets of Japan today. The crests of shop names or trade symbols are displayed on special curtains (called *noren*) and on the signs of old establishments. Some kamon tell what the shops sell, while others symbolize the business's tradition and good reputation. Restaurants, especially those that specialize in traditional Japanese cuisine, display crests to evoke a sense of long-time establishment and family ownership.

Even large companies and corporations sometimes adopt the founder's family crest to represent the entire company, and some local governments use crests to symbolize their communities.

The prevalence of kamon today seems to signify that they have found a permanent place in Japanese life and will survive as an important aspect of cultural identity, even in modern Japanese society. It is hoped that this book will provide an opportunity for people in and outside of Japan to know more about family crests, a precious cultural heritage left by Japan's ancestors.

All Japanese words in this book have been romanized in the Hepburn system, with macrons to indicate "long vowels," except for common place names.

The photos on these pages and elsewhere in this book depict examples of the way kamon are used on everyday objects in Japan. The kamon may not be immediately apparent, but look closely at each image and you will find a crest adorning each object. The circular form of the designs should help you find the crest.

Paper lantern of Kanda Shrine

End post of the wall of Sengen Shrine

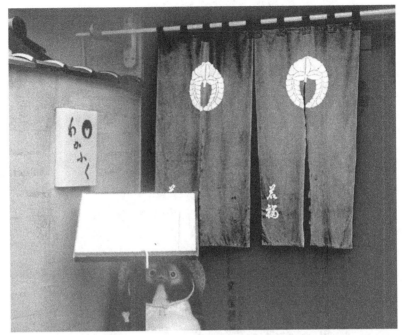

Shop curtains (*noren*)

Gable of a warehouse

The actors Kataoka Nizaemon VII and Sawamura Sōjūrō III in the roles of Ki no Natora and Kujaku Saburō, by Tōshūsai Sharaku (Ota Memorial Museum of Art)

Daimyō in ceremonial costume of *daimon* and *naga-bakama* trousers (The Costume Museum)

Painting of the Battle of Sekigahara on a folding screen (Gifu City Museum of History)

1. Crests and the Class System

There are several theories about how and when crests originated. The common belief, however, is that they were first used in the twelfth century by the noble class to decorate clothing and furniture.

Symbols or patterns adopted by members of the noble class were passed down to their descendants over generations. In this way, specific symbols and patterns were gradually established as each family's crest (*kamon*). During this time, crests were used mostly for decorative purposes, and their designs were often ornate and complicated. Some were made in commemoration of important events or special people.

Samurai (warrior) families began to use crests after the court nobles started the trend. Most of the samurai families' crests developed from symbols used on their battle flags and encampment curtains. In the Kamakura period (from the late twelfth to mid-fourteenth century), when different clans united and fought for influence and power, the samurai needed symbols to represent new coalitions and distinguish allies from enemies.

Because of the strict hierarchical nature of Japanese society during the Edo period (1603–1867), commoners were not formally permitted to have family crests until after the Meiji Restoration (in the latter half of the nineteenth century), when they began using surnames. However, the use of crests had already spread to the peasant, merchant, and artisan classes in the Edo period, much earlier than officially allowed. Rich commoners who had special permission to wear *haori* (kimono jackets) and *hakama* (full, pleated trousers) and carry *wakizashi* (short swords) had already begun to decorate their jackets and lanterns with family crests.

Some merchants, eager to make their shops conspicuous, displayed crests on their *noren* (shop curtains). Actors, public performers, and prostitutes also made use of kamon, employing them as personal trademarks. Farming villages would sometimes band together and form an association. The creation of a new design for the official crest of the new community was a very important part of the unification process.

II. Crests Through the Ages

Because the lineage of court nobles remained self-contained and relatively unbroken, the ruling class did not need to develop a wide variety of designs. On the other hand, in the much larger warrior class, family crests spread rapidly and extensively.

After the Kamakura shogunate was formed, a series of major battles among samurai families erupted. During this time, family crests were commonly used as symbols on flags, encampment curtains, and other battle paraphernalia. Some lords began to bestow official family crests to retainers who performed meritorious deeds. During the Nanbokuchō period (from the mid-fourteenth to mid-fifteenth century), family crests continued to increase in importance and authority for both court nobles and samurai, becoming potent symbols for families.

At first, each family was represented by a single kamon. However, in the Nanbokuchō and Muromachi periods (continuing through the first half of the sixteenth century), internal fighting caused samurai families to divide into competing factions. As these factions were established, they developed new designs to symbolize their allegiance, contributing to the increased use of family crests during these periods.

In the Edo period when wars were suppressed, flags and other battle-related items were no longer needed. During this relatively stable time, family crests were used mainly to enforce adherence to rules of conduct. For example, when *daimyō* (feudal lords) traveling to Edo Castle passed each other on the road, they were required to give an appropriate greeting in accordance with their relative positions in the social hierarchy. The lords often hired special retainers who were experts on kamon to help them identify an approaching *daimyō*.

Since the Edo period was an era of peace, people had more time to pursue leisure and luxury. Clothes in particular became much more extravagant and ornate than before, and family crests that had originally been symbols of family names were used simply for decoration. People sometimes modified or even replaced their original family crests, opting for something more elegant or refined. The kamon used by playboys were often altered considerably.

As altered crests became the norm, three new varieties of kamon came into fashion. *Date-mon* portrayed characters and pictures based on famous places and old poems. *Kaga-mon* incorporated color for the first time. *Hiyoku-mon* were those created by couples combining elements from their respective family crests.

The phenomenon of creating new crest styles and designs occurred not only among commoners, but also in the samurai class. As a result, the system of using a single design to represent each family line was thrown into confusion. After the Meiji Restoration, as traditional Japanese clothing was rapidly replaced by Western-style apparel, ceremonial clothing decorated with family crests went largely out of use.

III. DESIGN EVOLUTION

As a family prospered and its lineage expanded, it became necessary to distinguish between the main family and its branches, and also between legitimate and illegitimate children. To do this, the growing family modified its original crest to create a variety of related crests. Some of the basic techniques for altering kamon are addition, alteration, combination, and division.

Addition

The addition method involves introducing new stylistic elements into the original crest. There are two basic types of addition—adding something around the crest and adding something within the crest.

Adding Around

The most common method of addition is to make a circle or square frame around the crest. When families first started to use kamon on battle flags and encampment curtains, the crests' shape and size were not restricted. But in the Sengoku period (1467–1568), two formal kimono styles that displayed kamon were created. They were *suō* and *kataginu*. These kimono styles standardized the crests' shape and size, so crests were often enclosed in round or square frames.

1. Ring
2. Threadlike ring

3. Thin and thick rings
4. Double ring

3

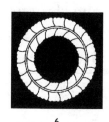
4

5. Bamboo circle
6. Wisteria circle

5

6

7. Square frame
8. Tiled square frame with cropped corners

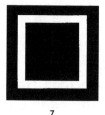
7

8

Adding Within

Adding something within the crest involves adding another picture or symbol to the original design. For example, adding *ken* (sword) to *katabami* (wood sorrel) yields the new design, *ken katabami*.
9. Wood sorrel and swords

9

Alteration

The alteration technique entails making more substantial changes to the original crest design. Some specific kinds of alteration include:

10

Shadowed (*kage*), Yin and Yang (*in'yo*)

The white and black parts of the design are reversed, creating a shadowed effect. The word *kage* (shadow) is added to the original name of the crest; for example, *tsuta* (ivy) would become *kage tsuta*. When the original design is placed next to the shadowed version, it is called *in'yo* (yin and yang).

10. Shadowed ivy

11

Front and Back (*omote, ura*)

Most kamon portray the front (*omote*) of objects. However, the design can be changed to show what the object looks like from behind. For these crests, the word *ura* (backside) is added to the original name; for example, *ura kikyō* (bellflower).

11. Backside-view bellflower

12

Single and Double (*tanpuku*)

Flowers depicted in crests are usually single-petaled, but some are double-petaled. In this case, *yae* (double-petaled) is added, as in *yae karahana* (Chinese flower).

12. Double-petaled Chinese flower

Imitating an Artistic Style

The original design is altered to imitate the style of a popular artist. The most common of these were the style of Ogata Kōrin, a Japanese painter in the mid-Edo period known for his decorative style. The name of this crest, for example, is *Kōrin ume*.

13. *Kōrin*-style plum blossom

13

Top View (*mukō*)

An object can be depicted as seen from above. An example is *mukō botan*.

14. Top-view peony

14

Side View (*yoko-mi*)

The motif is depicted as seen from the side; an example is *yoko-mi ume*.

15. Side-view plum blossom

15

Peephole View (*nozoki*)

The motif is only partially depicted, as if the object were viewed through a peephole. *Nozoki kikyō* is a good example.

16. Peephole-view bellflower in circle

16

17

Reshaping

The shape of the object is altered to resemble that of a different crest. For example, depicting a cherry blossom (*sakura*) in the shape of a butterfly (*chō*) results in *sakura chō*.

17. Butterfly-shaped cherry blossom

18

Other Types of Alteration

Twisting (*nejiri*)

18. Twisted chrysanthemum

19

Looping (*musubi*)

19. Looped wild goose

20

Folding (*ore*)

20. Folded hawk feather

Combination

As the name suggests, the combination technique creates a new crest by combining two or more motifs.

Facing (*mukai*)

Two like designs are placed symmetrically, facing each other; e.g., *mukai ichō*.
21. Facing gingko leaves

21

Embracing (*daki*)

Two crests which have a relatively long shape are portrayed facing each other, their lower parts crossing one or more times as if embracing; e.g., *daki tachibana*.
22. Embracing mandarins

22

Intersecting (*chigai*)

Two crests which have a relatively long shape are crossed in the center; e.g., *maru ni chigai takanoha*.
23. Intersecting hawk feathers, encircled

23

24

Parallel (*narabi*)

Two or more of the same crests are positioned side by side, parallel to each other; e.g., *sanmai narabi kashiwa*.
24. Three parallel oak leaves

25

Layered or Overlapping (*kasane*)

Crests are depicted in a layered or overlapping arrangement; e.g., *kasane i-geta*.
25. Overlapping well frames

26

27

Linked (*tsunagi*), With Child (*ko-mochi*)

26. Chain-linked circles

27. Embracing arrowheads with child (*ko-mochi*)

28

29

Other Types of Combination

Piled or stacked (*mori*)
28. Three piled wisteria blooms
Following, head-to-tail (*oi*)
29. Three head-to-tail paper mulberry leaves

Nested (*ire-ko*)

30. Wooden measures nested inside each other, encircled

30

Merging

Another possibility is that of combining two or more different designs. An example is *ichi-moji ni mitsu-domoe*.

31. Kanji numeral *ichi* (one) and three swirls

31

Division

The division method entails dividing a crest into two or more pieces, then rearranging them to create a new crest. This is one way to create a new crest design using the same basic motif. These divided crests are called *wari-mon*. An example is *mitsu-wari katabami*.

32. Trisected wood sorrels

32

IV. Distribution

In general, only one kamon per surname existed because the function of the crest was to symbolize the family name itself. However, crests were sometimes passed on to other families with different surnames in the following ways:

Bestowal

The family head could make a gift of his family crest to one of his retainers who had performed a meritorious deed, or to one who would carry on the family name through marriage.

Grant

A kamon was sometimes transferred between families within the same social class. This type of transfer was commonly used to ensure family-name succession through marriage.

Borrowing

Sometimes a family took the crest of another important, well-respected family and used it as their own. This was usually considered an honorable practice.

Capture

After defeating a rival, the victor often commandeered the enemy's crest. The enemy's kamon was celebrated as a symbol of the victory.

Because of all the various ways in which crests were transferred, it was not uncommon for a given surname to be represented by more than one crest. In these cases, it was necessary for the family to determine which symbol would officially represent its family name. The official crest for a surname was called *jō-mon* (regular crest) or *sei-mon* (official crest) and was used for official ceremonies and documents.

A crest did not necessarily become official just because it had been passed down through many generations. A crest received as a gift from an honorable lord or one representing successful military exploits often took precedence over the hereditary one and was used as the *sei-mon*.

To distinguish the official crest from all others, the unofficial crests were called *kae-mon* (alternative crest), *fuku-mon* (second crest), *ura-mon* (extra crest), etc. They could not be used in official situations.

V. Widespread Adoption

As eras changed and trends evolved, crests came to be used for a surprisingly wide variety of purposes.

Clothes

It was rare for court nobles to decorate their clothes with kamon, but samurai families in the Kamakura period (late twelfth to mid-fourteenth century) made the practice popular. When samurai started adorning their *hitatare* (traditional clothing) with crests in the Nanbokuchō period (mid-fourteenth to mid-fifteenth century), decorating formal garments with family crests gradually became an accepted custom.

Daimon, a special kind of *hitatare* marked prominently with kamon, became the accepted formal wear among samurai in the Muromachi period (from the early fourteenth to the first half of the sixteenth century). *Daimon* had five crests on the jacket and five on the *hakama* (trousers), all of which were left black and white without color embellishments.

Around the mid-Edo period (circa mid-eighteenth century), the *haori-hakama*, which had five crests emblazoned on the back, front, and sleeves, became the preferred formal wear for men. They were approved as official garments in the mid-nineteenth century, and still remain in use in modern Japan.

Buildings

Crests were displayed on roof tiles in the Nanbokuchō period, and were used as a design element throughout buildings in the Sengoku period (1467–1568). The legendary Toyotomi Hideyoshi, Japan's greatest rags-to-riches figure, put his paulownia crest on tiles, indoor decorations, clothing, and furnishings within his castles.

Shrines and temples also began using crests during this period. They usually adopted the crests of powerful clans in return for financial support, although some shrines kept the traditional crest that represented their patron god.

Osaka Castle

It became the norm for samurai families to display family crests on castles and residences in the Edo period (1603–1867). Gradually the trend spread to the lower classes. Particularly in Edo (the former name of Tokyo), businesses, stores, and warehouses used crests to represent the company or owner, similar to how businesses today use trademarks.

Ships

It was common in the Edo period to put family crests on the sails and banners of ships. When the feudal lords from western regions of the country made their journey to Edo to fulfill the *sankin kotai* (a require-ment to attend the court in Edo for a full year, every other year), they often came in ships, which prominently displayed their family crests.

Gravestones and Mortuary Tablets

In the Insei era (mid-eleventh to late twelfth century), patterns were sometimes carved on gravestones. In the Sengoku period, when Christianity spread, the cross was often carved on the gravestones of Christians.

Gravestone

In the Edo period, it became popular to carve family crests on gravestones. On a woman's gravestone, the crests of both her husband and her parents were often displayed side by side.

Battle Gear

On the battlefield, family crests were emblazoned on armor, shields, bow sheaths, and quivers. The designs helped warriors distinguish enemies from allies, and made for good fashion as well.

VI. Symbolism and Meaning

As more and more families and businesses began to use crests, the number of designs and motifs greatly increased, and the ways in which they were selected became complex. Each crest developed its own symbolic meaning over the years, and families chose an appropriate design based on the meaning of the symbols. There were seven classifications of symbolism that were considered when choosing a crest.

Patterns

Many crests originated from decorative patterns. Court nobles favored them because their designs were elegant. Most of these patterns were based on plant motifs, in contrast to the animal designs preferred by samurai.

Family Name Symbolism

Some crests were chosen because of their connection to certain surnames. The correlations between crests and names were either direct or indirect. Two good examples of a direct relationship are the *sakura* (cherry blossom) crest used by the Sakurai family, and the *torii* (shrine gate) crest used by the Torii clan. An example of an indirect link between a family name and a crest is the case of the Yoshino family, which adopted the *sakura* pattern because the town of Yoshino (in Nara) is famous for cherry blossoms.

Auspicious Symbolism

Kamon sometimes represent a family's wish for good fortune, longevity, good health, prosperity, happiness, or property. Some crests express this directly through kanji characters, such as: 天 (*ten*, heaven), 長 (*chō*, long), 大 (*dai*, big), 福 (*fuku*, fortune), 寿 (*kotobuki*, happiness), or 吉 (*kichi*, good luck). Other families chose pictorial designs that symbolized good fortune, such as the paulownia, on which the auspicious Chinese phoenix is said to perch.

Commemoration

A symbolic kamon design was sometimes adopted to commemorate an ancestor's origin or heroic deed. For example, legend says that when the Nanbu clan fought against the Akita clan, two cranes landed in the Nanbus' encampment, and after this, the Nanbu clan was victorious in the battle. So the Nanbu clan adopted the pattern of a pair of cranes as its family crest to commemorate the event.

Martial Spirit

Samurai families often took the elegant crests of court nobles and altered them in a way that expressed their fighting spirit. One possible method was adding weapons such as swords, armor, or bows and arrows. Sometimes kamon depicting brave animals like hawks, lions, or tigers were adopted.

Religious Symbolism

Some crests were based on religious symbolism related to Shintō, Buddhism, Christianity, or Confucianism. Kamon were developed in spiritual and superstitious eras when deities were very influential in people's lives. People prayed earnestly to their gods or Buddhas and asked for their protection. Many crests expressing religious beliefs were created particularly in the Sengoku period.

Shintō

Since ancient times, the Japanese have believed in the existence of a great number of gods and goddesses. The worship of war gods was prevalent in the age of samurai rule. Warriors worshiped Hachiman (or Yawata), the deity of the bow and arrow, as well as others such as Kumano Gongen, Suwa Myōjin, and Kamo Myōjin. The devotees of these gods adopted sacred animals, plants, or heavenly bodies as their crests.

Buddhism

Some crests symbolize faith in Buddhism. Examples include the *rinpō* (Dharma Chakra), which is said to destroy all hardships; the tin crosiers which ascetics carry to punish evil; the Myōken Bosatsu (a symbol of the Big Dipper); the three "general stars" which preside over weapons; the swastika; the kanji character 無 (*mu*, meaning "nothing"); and the symbol which represented karma.

Christianity

Christianity was first introduced to Japan in the mid-sixteenth century, and its practice proliferated from Kyushu through Ōshū. However, since Toyotomi Hideyoshi outlawed its practice, there are only a few crests related to Christianity. These crests depict the cross, either directly or in disguise. The Ikeda clan wanted to express their Christian beliefs, but were afraid to display the cross openly, so they chose the Gion *mamori* (talisman), a Shintō good-luck charm from the Gion Shrine that bears a resemblance to the cross.

Confucianism

Confucianism was brought to Japan from China in ancient times, but there are only a few crests related to this philosophy. One example is the *hakke*, the eight patterns of divining sticks from the *I Ching* (Book of Changes), a fortune-telling book thought to have been composed in the Zhou period in China. Another is the *tai ji* diagram, which Zhou Dun'yi illustrated during the Song Dynasty to depict the formation and development of all things based on the theory of yin-yang and the five elements.

Superstitious Symbolism

Long ago, when superstition was an integral part of life, people tried to cure illness and bring good luck by using charms and talismans. They sometimes adopted these talismans as their crests. The motifs of these crests include the *jūmonji* (crisscross), Abeno Seimei's seal (the pentagram-like seal of a legendary doctor), and the *kagome* (basket).

VII. Motifs

Heaven and Earth Crests

Motifs depicting astronomical bodies and atmospheric phenomena belong to the category of heaven and earth crests.

The Sun (*hi* or *hinomaru*)

Crests modeled after the sun were not often used as family crests. In the latter part of the Edo period, Japanese ships entering the sea near Japan began raising the *hinomaru* (rising-sun flag) to distinguish themselves from foreign ships. Later, *hinomaru* came to be used as the national flag of Japan.

33

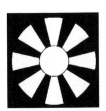

34

35

33. Sunbeams
34. Eight-rayed sun
35. Rising sun with rays

36

37

36. Rising sun
37. Sunbeams and running water

The Moon (*tsuki*)

Crests modeled after the moon have several names, depending on the shape or brightness of the moon depicted such as *mika-zuki* (new moon), *han-getsu* (half-moon), *man-getsu* (full moon), and *oboro-zuki* (hazy moon). They were probably adopted as family crests for religious reasons. The devotees of Myōken Bosatsu* (or Sudarsti, a Bodhisattva) often used these crests.

Moreover, because a half-moon looks like a bow with a string, it is also called *gen-getsu* (string moon) or *yumihari-zuki* (stretched-bow moon). Thus, the design was sometimes chosen to express the samurai spirit.

38. Half-moon
39. Hazy moon for the Ōzeki family
40. Moon and rabbit

41. Moon and cuckoo

38

39

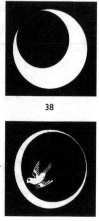

40

41

*The belief in Myōken is thought to have begun in the early Heian period (794–1185). Myōken was worshiped as a war god, mostly by samurai.

The Moon and Stars (*tsuki-boshi*)

The moon and stars were worshiped by ancient people as powerful heavenly bodies. Buddhists referred to the Big Dipper as *Hokushin* (the north dragon), believing that it protected their country and helped relieve people's suffering. The Bodhisattva Myōken was referred to as the incarnation of that constellation.

42

43

44

42. Moon and star
43. Upward-facing moon and star
44. Moon and Big Dipper

Three Stars (*mitsu-boshi*)

The three stars represent the three fixed stars of Orion's belt, which have had various symbolic meanings through the years. Because they were called "three warriors" or "general stars" in China, they became important designs for warrior families.

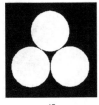
45

46

47

45. Three stars
46. Three stars, encircled
47. Three stars in rice cake

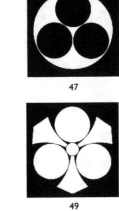
48   49

48. Three stars in snow wheel
49. Three swords and stars

Seven Stars (*shichiyō*)

Seven-star crests were modeled after the Big Dipper, and like *tsuki-boshi*, were based on the belief in Myōken.

50. Seven stars
51. Seven stars, encircled
52. Seven stars in rice cake

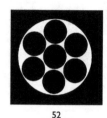

50　　　51　　　52

Nine Stars (*kuyō*)

The nine stars were originally used for fortune-telling in ancient India; later, Buddhists modeled nine Buddhas after these stars and worshiped them as the gods that protected all the earth. *Kuyō* was used as a pattern for clothes, palanquins, and oxcarts in the Heian period (794–1185), and was also the symbol of a prayer for safety and protection.

53. Nine stars
54. Nine stars, encircled
55. Nine stars, shadowed

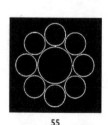

53　　　54　　　55

56. Square of nine stars
57. Rhombus of nine stars
58. Nine divided stars

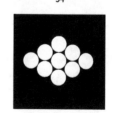

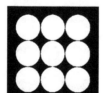

56　　　57　　　58

Cloud (*kumo*)

The cloud seen in crests is referred to as *zuiun*, meaning a cloud that appears as a lucky omen. Cloud patterns were imported with Buddhism and were later developed into crests. They were often used as temple kamon.

59

60

61

59. Cloud
60. Lucky cloud
61. Rhombic cloud

62

62. Two cloud swirls

Mist (*kasumi*)

The mist pattern never appears by itself, but rather is used as a background for a mountain or the moon.

63

63. Moon in the mist

Mountain (*yama*)

Certain mountains have been worshiped as gods since ancient times, and their beauty has been the object of awe and admiration, thus they came to be used as kamon designs.

64. Mount Fuji for the Aoki family
65. Distant mountain, encircled
66. Three mountains

64

65

66

Waves (*nami*)

Waves were first used as patterns in the Fujiwara period (897–1185), and they later became motifs for crests. Though they are elegant, samurai often used wave crests because they symbolized battle. The waves' persistent motion of crashing onto the shore and returning back to the sea evoked the charge and retreat of battle.

67. Standing waves
68. Swirled facing waves
69. Swirled waves, clockwise

67

68

69

70. Three swirled waves
71. Swirled facing waves and plovers
72. Shadowed overlapping waves

70

71

72

Snow (*yuki*)

The pure white, six-pointed snowflake has long been admired as a thing of beauty. The snow, moon, and flowers (*setsu-getsu-ka*) hold a special place in Japanese culture as representatives of seasonal beauty. Besides adding beauty to winter scenery, snow is also regarded as a harbinger of a good harvest in the coming year.

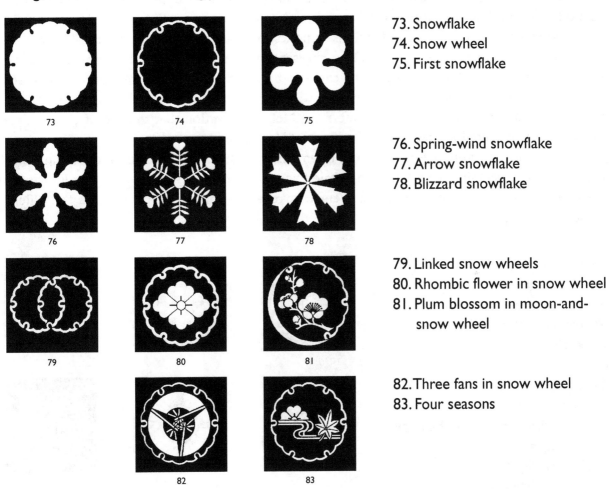

73. Snowflake
74. Snow wheel
75. First snowflake

76. Spring-wind snowflake
77. Arrow snowflake
78. Blizzard snowflake

79. Linked snow wheels
80. Rhombic flower in snow wheel
81. Plum blossom in moon-and-snow wheel

82. Three fans in snow wheel
83. Four seasons

Plant Crests

Plant motifs are the most prevalent in Japanese family crests.

Chrysanthemum (*kiku*)

Chrysanthemums had a special role in ancient Chinese culture. People not only admired the beautiful blooms, but also used them as medicinal herbs to promote longevity. After the idea was introduced into Japan, chrysanthemums came to be regarded as the noblest of all flowers.

The emperor Gotoba enjoyed using the chrysanthemum pattern, and the three succeeding emperors followed suit; thus, the pattern came to be reserved for Imperial Household crests. The design, however, was sometimes granted to other persons for their distinguished service to the Imperial Household. It was only after the Meiji Restoration that the use of chrysanthemum crests was officially reserved for the Imperial Household.

The crest for the Imperial Family is the open design with sixteen double petals, while other royalty use the backside-view fourteen-petaled version (although each royal family informally uses another chrysanthemum design). Even today the chrysanthemum is used as the official crest for the Imperial Household.

84. Sixteen-petaled chrysanthemum
85. Bisected chrysanthemums
86. Trisected chrysanthemums, encircled

87. Three side-view chrysanthemums
88. Quadrisected chrysanthemums and square flowers
89. Thousand-petaled chrysanthemum

84

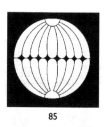
85

86

87

88

89

90. Chrysanthemum and water
91. Half-chrysanthemum and kanji numeral *ichi* (one)
92. Two half-chrysanthemums, encircled

93. Rhombic chrysanthemum
94. Three rhombic chrysanthemums
95. Three piled rhombic chrysanthemums

96. *Gyōyō*-style chrysanthemum
97. Side-view chrysanthemum between two leaves
98. Trisected chrysanthemum and leaves in tortoiseshell

99. Embracing chrysanthemum leaves
100. Three chrysanthemum leaves
101. Chrysanthemum between half-leaves

102. Chrysanthemum branch circle
103. Chrysanthemum branch
104. Chrysanthemum petals in disarray

105. Crane-shaped chrysanthemum
106. Butterfly-shaped chrysanthemum
107. Boat-shaped chrysanthemum

108. Wood sorrel leaves and swords in *fusen*-style* chrysanthemum wheel

105

106

107

108

Paulownia (*kiri*)

A deciduous tree of the figwort family, the paulownia has light purple flowers that bloom around May. Its wood is light and easy to work with, so it is a popular material for furniture such as chests.

The paulownia was adopted as a crest motif because it is a symbol of good fortune. In ancient China, paulownias were considered to be lucky trees where phoenixes lived. In the Chinese poetry collection, *Anthology of Bai Juyi*, there is a poem in which a phoenix lives in the high branches of a blooming paulownia and sings, "Long live the king!" Thus, paulownia patterns came to be used for the emperor's garments, and later as crests at the end of the Kamakura period.

The Imperial Court bestowed the paulownia crests to retainers such as Ashikaga Takauji, and later the Ashikagas gave the crests to vassals who had performed meritorious deeds, such as Oda Nobunaga. Toyotomi Hideyoshi, who had also been allowed to use paulownia crests, distributed them so often that even people to whom they had not been given started using them.

*Fusen (ryō)
This term originally referred to a diagonal cloth woven into a design. It now describes both an arabesque pattern with petals in the corners and a special pattern in the shape of a butterfly with wings spread.

Though Hideyoshi prohibited the use of both chrysanthemum and paulownia crests, the ban had little effect and quite a number of *daimyō* used these patterns during the Edo period. Tokugawa Ieyasu was another notable figure who was allowed to use this popular crest, but he refused it and used a hollyhock design instead.

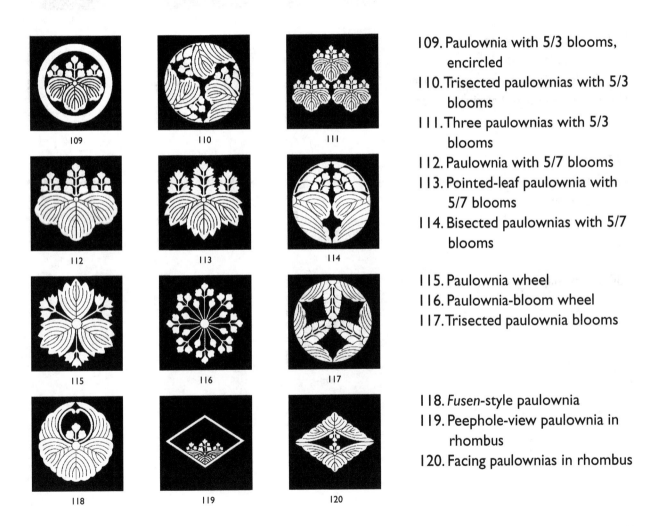

109

110

111

112

113

114

115

116

117

118

119

120

109. Paulownia with 5/3 blooms, encircled
110. Trisected paulownias with 5/3 blooms
111. Three paulownias with 5/3 blooms
112. Paulownia with 5/7 blooms
113. Pointed-leaf paulownia with 5/7 blooms
114. Bisected paulownias with 5/7 blooms

115. Paulownia wheel
116. Paulownia-bloom wheel
117. Trisected paulownia blooms

118. *Fusen*-style paulownia
119. Peephole-view paulownia in rhombus
120. Facing paulownias in rhombus

121. Paulownia blossoms
122. Dancing paulownia
123. *Kōrin*-style paulownia

121

122

123

124. Seven paulownia leaves, encircled
125. Paulownia blossoms in disarray
126. Paulownia with hanging flowers

124

125

124

125

126

127. Heron-shaped paulownia
128. Shadowed butterfly-shaped paulownia
129. Bat-shaped paulownia

127

128

129

130. Boat-shaped paulownia

130

Hollyhock (*aoi*)

Though usually translated as hollyhock, *aoi* crests were actually modeled after the leaves (and sometimes flowers) of a slightly different perennial plant of the birthwort family, also called *futaba-aoi* or *kamo-aoi*.

Though the origin of the crest is uncertain, it is said that some court nobles used the young leaves of hollyhocks to decorate their clothes, carts, horses, etc., during the "Hollyhock Festival," a Shintō ritual at the Kamo Shrine in Kyoto. Hollyhocks thereafter became associated with the gods worshiped there. Devotees of these deities sanctified hollyhocks and began using them as their crests. Hollyhock crests are an example of kamon selected for their religious symbolism.

When Tokugawa Ieyasu became the first shōgun of the Edo Bakufu, his use of the hollyhock crest made it superior to both the chrysanthemum and paulownia, the motifs traditionally used by the emperors before him. During the ensuing Edo period, only the Tokugawa family was permitted to use the hollyhock design.

131. Two-leaf hollyhock
132. Standing hollyhock and water
133. Standing hollyhock, encircled

134. Trisected standing hollyhocks
135. Three hollyhocks in vine circle
136. Three hollyhocks and swords

137. Trisected hollyhocks
138. Facing hollyhocks with flowers
139. Trisected hollyhocks with flowers

    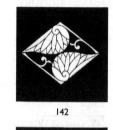

137   138   139

140. Five hollyhocks
141. Rhombic standing hollyhocks
142. Rhombic bisected hollyhocks with vine

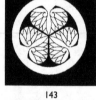 

140   141   142

143. Three hollyhocks for the Tokugawa family
144. Bundled hollyhocks for the Honda family
145. *Fusen*-style hollyhock

143   144   145

146. Hollyhock circle
147. Hollyhock in vine circle
148. Three hollyhocks with vines

146   147   148

149. Wheel of six hollyhocks
150. Paulownia-shaped hollyhock

149   150

Wisteria (*fuji*)

The wisteria is a deciduous shrub of the legume family. These crests were modeled after the shape of the wisteria's leaves and blossoms. People have enjoyed wisteria blooms since the Nara period (710–94), and there are poems about them in the anthology *Man'yoshu* (Collection of Ten Thousand Leaves). Wisteria bloom-viewing feasts were common. The plant was also frequently used as a pattern for clothes, which were illustrated in *Eiga Monogatari* (The Glory Story) and *Genji Monogatari* (The Tale of Genji). After that, the pattern was altered into a crest design, and families that have the kanji for wisteria in their names often adopted this kamon.

151. Climbing wisteria
152. Hanging wisteria, encircled
153. Rhombic climbing wisteria

154. Wisteria bloom
155. Three wisteria blooms with leaves
156. Three wisteria blooms with vines

157. Six wisterias
158. Two wisterias
159. Three wisterias

160. Swirled wisteria
161. Two swirled wisterias
162. Three swirled wisterias

 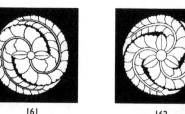 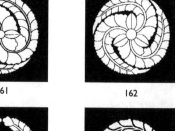

160   161   162

163. Three swirls in hanging
    wisteria
164. Sickle in climbing wisteria
165. Rhombic flower in wisteria
    ring

163   164   165

166. Wisteria ring
167. Wisteria wheel
168. Wisteria branch circle

166   167   168

169. Circle of hanging wisterias
    and branches
170. Two wisteria branches in
    shape of rhombus
171. *Gyōyō*-style wisteria bloom
    with leaves
172. Paulownia-shaped wisteria
173. Butterfly-shaped wisteria

169   170   171

172   173

Gentian (*rindō*)

Gentians, perennial plants of the gentian family, have been admired by people since the Fujiwara period. They appear in both *Genji Monogatari* and *Makura no Sōshi* (The Pillow Book of Sei Shōnagon). These plants were first depicted in decorative patterns, and then were made into kamon designs. These crests were used mostly by court nobles.

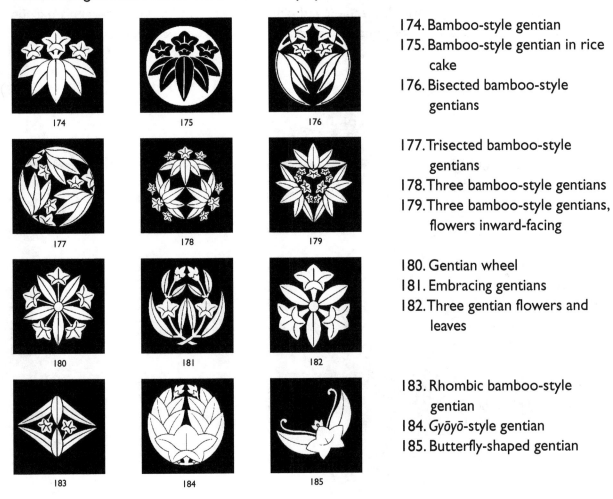

174. Bamboo-style gentian
175. Bamboo-style gentian in rice cake
176. Bisected bamboo-style gentians

177. Trisected bamboo-style gentians
178. Three bamboo-style gentians
179. Three bamboo-style gentians, flowers inward-facing

180. Gentian wheel
181. Embracing gentians
182. Three gentian flowers and leaves

183. Rhombic bamboo-style gentian
184. *Gyōyō*-style gentian
185. Butterfly-shaped gentian

Japanese Plum (*ume*)

The *ume* is a small deciduous tree of the rose family. Crests that depict its blossom in a realistic style are called *ume*, while those that portray it in a geometrical pattern are called *umebachi*, meaning, "*ume* bowl." Plum blossoms, along with pines and bamboos, became an auspicious symbol because of their resistance to cold weather. They were used as patterns for clothing and other household items. Sugawara Michizane loved plum blossoms, and it is said that this may be the reason they were used for religious crests at the Tenmangū shrines, where Michizane was deified.

186. Plum blossom
187. Top-view plum blossom
188. Three plum blossoms and
     leaves, top view

189. Double-flowered plum
     blossom
190. Shadowed double-petaled
     top-view plum blossom
191. Twisted plum blossom

192. Bottom-view plum blossom
193. Trisected plum blossoms
194. Three piled plum blossoms

186   187   188
189   190   191
192   193   194

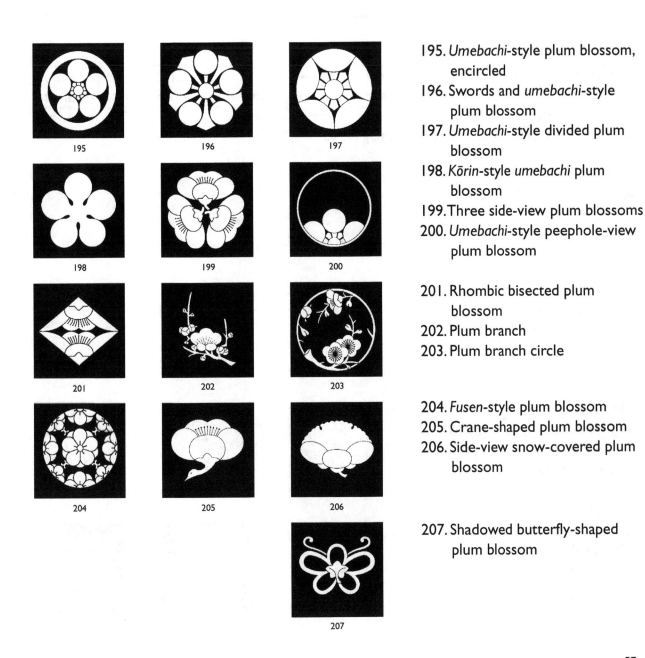

195. *Umebachi*-style plum blossom, encircled
196. Swords and *umebachi*-style plum blossom
197. *Umebachi*-style divided plum blossom
198. *Kōrin*-style *umebachi* plum blossom
199. Three side-view plum blossoms
200. *Umebachi*-style peephole-view plum blossom

201. Rhombic bisected plum blossom
202. Plum branch
203. Plum branch circle

204. *Fusen*-style plum blossom
205. Crane-shaped plum blossom
206. Side-view snow-covered plum blossom

207. Shadowed butterfly-shaped plum blossom

Peony (*botan*)

A deciduous shrub of the peony family, this plant was introduced from China, where people used the petals for food and the roots for medicine in addition to appreciating the colorful blooms. The Japanese also admired the peony, which was first used in patterns for clothes and oxcarts, and later became a motif for family crests.

208. Standing peony
209. Twisted peony
210. Backside-view peony

211. Embracing peony
212. Fallen peony
213. Pile of three fallen peonies

214. *Gyōyō*-style peony
215. Intersecting peony leaves, encircled
216. Five peony leaves

217. Intersecting peonies
218. Head-to-tail peonies, encircled
219. Peony branch

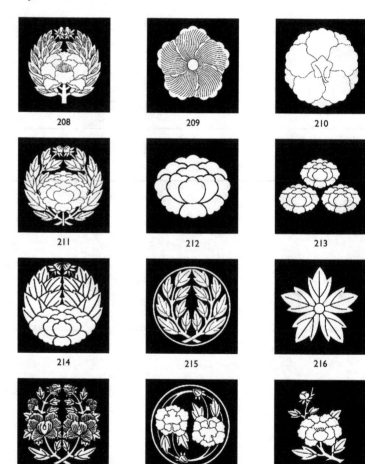

208

209

210

211

212

213

214

215

216

217

218

219

220

221

222

223

224

225

226

227

228

220. Facing peonies in shape of rhombus
221. Fallen peony in rhombus, peephole-view
222. *Fusen*-style peony

223. Peony and demon
224. Peony and butterfly
225. Crane-shaped peony

226. Paulownia-shaped peony
227. Crab-shaped peony
228. Peony for the Nabeshima family

Bellflower (*kikyō*)

The perennial bellflower produces beautiful indigo-blue flowers from summer to autumn. The flower was used as a family crest simply for its beauty, although the crest also held symbolic meaning for the Toki clan. According to legend, an ancestor of the Toki clan picked a bellflower to put on his armor at a time of war, then proceeded to win the battle. Thus, the family adopted the flower for their family crest to commemorate the event.

As a matter of historical interest, the pale-blue bellflower is the family crest of Akechi Mitsuhide, who defeated Oda Nobunaga at Honnōji temple just before Nobunaga could succeed in unifying the nation.

229. Bellflower
230. Bellflower in rice cake
231. Double-flowered bellflower

229

230

231

232. Side-view bellflower
233. *Kōrin*-style bellflower
234. Twisted bellflower

232

233

234

235. Looped bellflower
236. Three piled bellflowers
237. Bellflower and swords

235

236

237

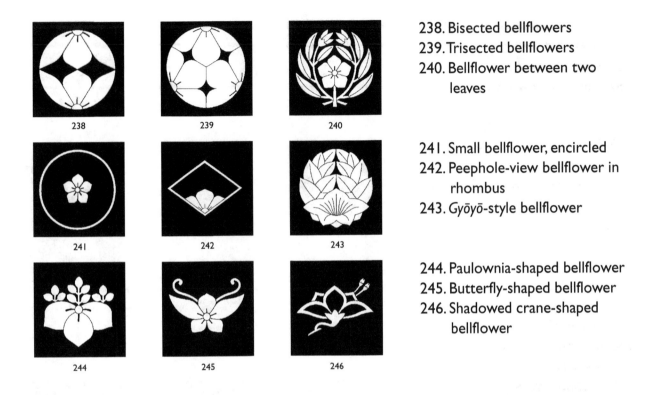

238. Bisected bellflowers
239. Trisected bellflowers
240. Bellflower between two leaves

241. Small bellflower, encircled
242. Peephole-view bellflower in rhombus
243. *Gyōyō*-style bellflower

244. Paulownia-shaped bellflower
245. Butterfly-shaped bellflower
246. Shadowed crane-shaped bellflower

Wood Sorrel (*katabami*)

A perpetual of the oxalis family, the wood sorrel seems to have been used in patterns because of its elegant shape, although another view holds that it was chosen for its fecundity.

247. Wood sorrel
248. Wood sorrel and swords, encircled
249. Double-flowered wood sorrel

250. Four-petaled wood sorrel, encircled
251. Twisted wood sorrel
252. Three piled wood sorrels

250   251   252

253. Shadowed looped wood sorrel
254. Shadowed *Kōrin*-style wood sorrel
255. Vine in shape of wood sorrel

253   254   255

256. Trisected wood sorrels, encircled
257. Trisected wood sorrels in shape of tortoiseshell
258. Trisected wood sorrels and swords
259. Peephole-view wood sorrel in circle
260. Wood sorrel in rhombus
261. Rhombic bisected wood sorrel

256   257   258

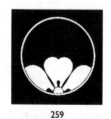  

259   260   261

262. Scale-shaped wood sorrel and swords
263. Fan-shaped wood sorrel
264. Butterfly-shaped wood sorrel and swords

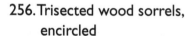  

262   263   264

Arrowhead (*omodaka*)

The arrowhead, a perpetual plant of the water plantain family, was also called *shōgunsō* (victorious army grass). Because of this martial connotation, it was a design favored for the crests of samurai families.

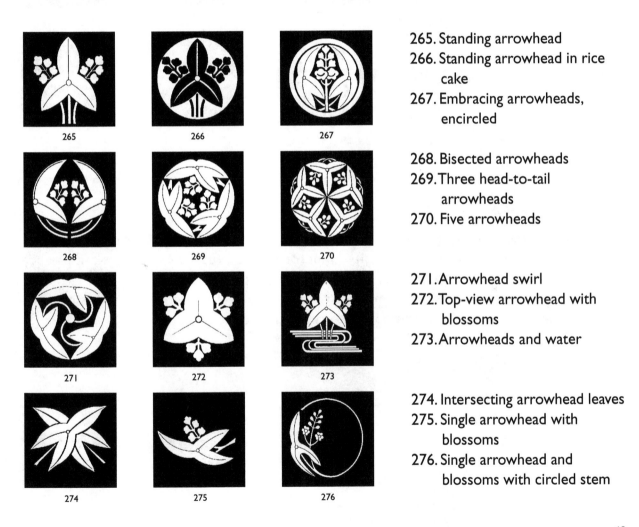

265. Standing arrowhead
266. Standing arrowhead in rice cake
267. Embracing arrowheads, encircled

268. Bisected arrowheads
269. Three head-to-tail arrowheads
270. Five arrowheads

271. Arrowhead swirl
272. Top-view arrowhead with blossoms
273. Arrowheads and water

274. Intersecting arrowhead leaves
275. Single arrowhead with blossoms
276. Single arrowhead and blossoms with circled stem

277. Rhombic facing arrowheads
278. *Fusen*-style arrowhead
279. Wheel of arrowheads

277

278

279

280. Paulownia-shaped arrowhead
281. Butterfly-shaped arrowhead
282. Crane-shaped arrowhead

280

281

282

Mandarin (*tachibana*)

The mandarin tree is an evergreen of the rue family. In a historical fable, it is referred to as the sacred tree planted in the land of eternity. Emperor Genmei (661–721, in the Nara period) loved this plant dearly and gave the name Tachibana to the prince, Katsuragi Oh. The Tachibana clan then adopted the plant as their family crest. Mandarin blossoms were also used as patterns in the Fujiwara period, and later developed into family crest designs.

283. Encircled mandarin
284. Shadowed mandarin
285. Vertically facing mandarins

283

284

285

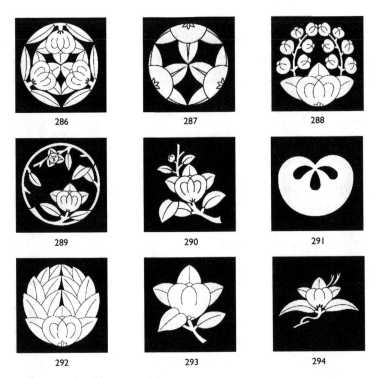

286. Circle of three mandarins
287. Top-view trisected mandarins
288. Mandarin blooms

289. Mandarin circle
290. Mandarin branch
291. *Kōrin*-style mandarin branch

292. *Gyōyō*-style mandarin
293. Fan-shaped mandarin
294. Crane-shaped mandarin

Oak (*kashiwa*)

It is believed that the leaves of these deciduous trees were used as platters to offer food to the gods. The tree came to be revered, and families that had been admitted to the Shintō priesthood often used it for their kamon.

295. Three oak leaves
296. Oak leaves and vines, encircled
297. Three oak leaves and swords, encircled

298. Three oak leaves in rhombus
299. Peephole-view oak leaves, encircled
300. Trisected oak leaves

301. Five oak leaves, encircled
302. Three swirled oak leaves
303. Facing oak leaves and rhombic flower

304. Three double oak leaves
305. Single oak leaf, encircled
306. Two parallel oak leaves, encircled

307. Embracing oak leaves
308. Intersecting oak leaves
309. Folded oak leaf, encircled

310. Crane-shaped oak leaves
311. Paulownia-shaped oak leaves
312. Shadowed bat-shaped oak leaves

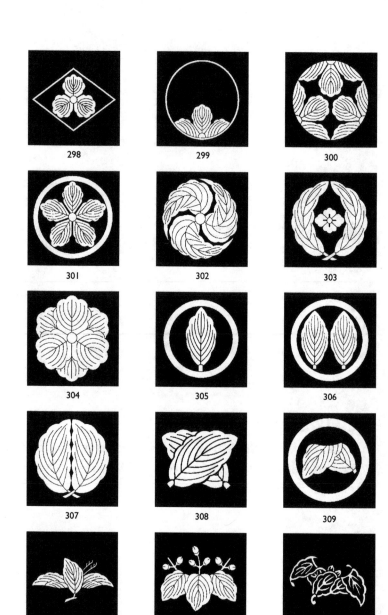

298
299
300
301
302
303
304
305
306
307
308
309
310
311
312

Paper Mulberry (*kaji*)

A deciduous tree of the mulberry family, the paper mulberry also had leaves that were used to offer food to the gods. They were depicted in patterns on the clothes of Shintō priests, and eventually they were established as religious crests.

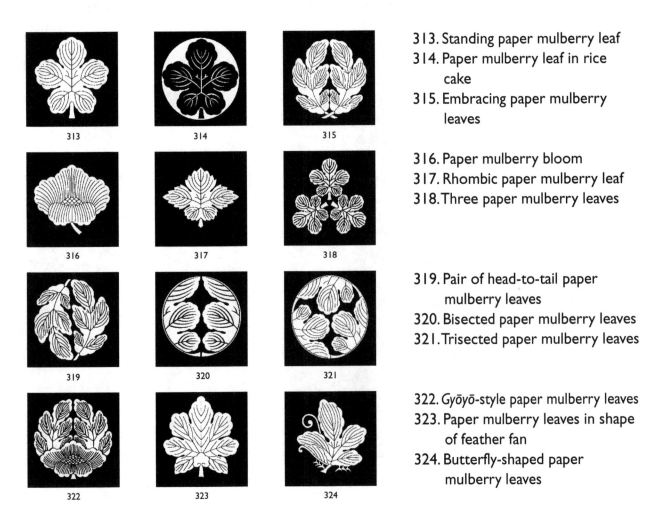

313. Standing paper mulberry leaf
314. Paper mulberry leaf in rice cake
315. Embracing paper mulberry leaves

316. Paper mulberry bloom
317. Rhombic paper mulberry leaf
318. Three paper mulberry leaves

319. Pair of head-to-tail paper mulberry leaves
320. Bisected paper mulberry leaves
321. Trisected paper mulberry leaves

322. *Gyōyō*-style paper mulberry leaves
323. Paper mulberry leaves in shape of feather fan
324. Butterfly-shaped paper mulberry leaves

Myōga

A perpetual of the ginger family, this plant is sometimes translated as "Japanese ginger." *Myōga* is homophonic with another word that means "blessings from the gods," so it has long been considered auspicious. People who adopted *myōga* as their kamon probably hoped to invoke good fortune. *Myōga* crests look similar to *gyōyō* crests, so they are sometimes confused.

325. Embracing *myōga*
326. Shadowed embracing *myōga*, Kōrin-style
327. *Myōga* circle

328. Circle of *myōga* and vines
329. Three intersecting *myōga*
330. Three *myōga*

331. Pair of head-to-tail *myōga*
332. Intersecting *myōga*
333. Pile of three embracing *myōga*

334. Three *myōga* swirls
335. Paulownia-shaped *myōga*
336. *Myōga* with blossom

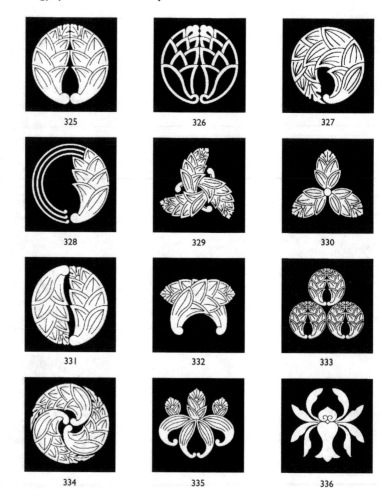

325   326   327
328   329   330
331   332   333
334   335   336

337. Rhombic embracing *myōga*
338. Three blooming *myōga*
339. Circle of *myōga* and branch

340. Wood sorrel in embracing *myōga* circle
341. Butterfly-shaped *myōga*

Pine (*matsu*)

These evergreens have been used in religious ceremonies and considered auspicious since ancient times. *Kadomatsu* (New Year's decorations made of pine branches) are still displayed at the gates and entryways of Japanese homes at New Year's. Since the Heian period, pine patterns have been used on oxcarts and other items; later, they became family crests.

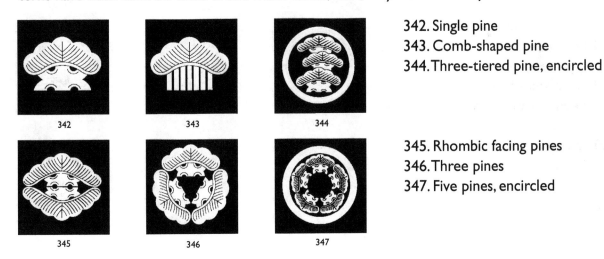

342. Single pine
343. Comb-shaped pine
344. Three-tiered pine, encircled

345. Rhombic facing pines
346. Three pines
347. Five pines, encircled

348. Embracing pine saplings
349. Six pine saplings
350. Shadowed rhombic pine bark

 348

 349

 350

351. Rhombic pine bark in rice cake
352. Pinecone with needles
353. Pine needles in shape of well frame

 351

 352

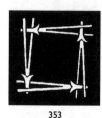 353

354. Rhombic pine needles
355. Pine needles in shape of three swirls
356. Peephole-view bellflower in rhombic pine needles

 354

 355

 356

357. *Torii* in swirled pine needles
358. Pine needles in shape of wood sorrel
359. Paulownia-shaped pine needles and cones

 357

 358

 359

360. Rhombus of pine and bamboo leaves
361. Three scale-shaped pines
362. *Kōrin*-style pine

 360

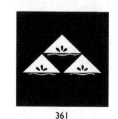 361

 362

Bamboo (*take, sasa*)

Evergreens of the grass family, *take* and *sasa* are two different species, but are often confused. Generally, smaller types of *take* (bamboo) are called *sasa*. According to Chinese legend, the phoenix ate bamboo fruit. It is probably this story that caused bamboo to be regarded as a lucky plant. Bamboo designs were first used as decorative patterns and later became family crests.

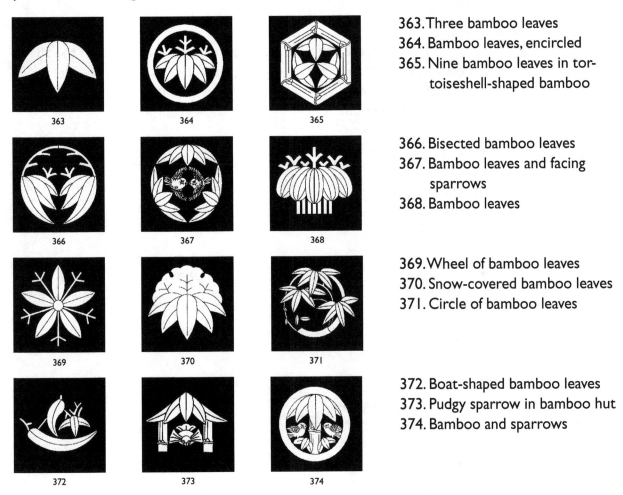

363. Three bamboo leaves
364. Bamboo leaves, encircled
365. Nine bamboo leaves in tortoiseshell-shaped bamboo

366. Bisected bamboo leaves
367. Bamboo leaves and facing sparrows
368. Bamboo leaves

369. Wheel of bamboo leaves
370. Snow-covered bamboo leaves
371. Circle of bamboo leaves

372. Boat-shaped bamboo leaves
373. Pudgy sparrow in bamboo hut
374. Bamboo and sparrows

375. Three bamboo pieces, encircled
376. Three interlocking bamboo rings
377. Bamboo and sedge hat

375

376

377

Japanese Cedar (*sugi*)

An evergreen of the genus *Cryptomeria*, the cedar has been deified as a sacred tree in the Shintō tradition because of its enormity and solemnity. Patterns using this tree were usually adopted as family crests for religious reasons. On the other hand, the Uesugi clan, the Sugi clan, and others who had *sugi* in their family names were also known to adopt these kamon.

378. Japanese cedar, encircled
379. Three Japanese cedars
380. Bisected Japanese cedars

378

379

380

381. Two Japanese cedars, peep-hole-view
382. Five-tiered Japanese cedars, encircled
383. Swirled Japanese cedars

381

382

383

384. Three Japanese cedars, head-to-tail
385. Rhombic bisected Japanese cedars
386. Rhombic Japanese cedar

384

385

386

Rice Plant (*ine*)

Since ancient times, rice was a form of currency for the Japanese, so it was held in very high regard. It seems that the rice plant was used as a kamon because of its symbolism as a good omen. Many Inari shrines, found all over Japan, use this crest.

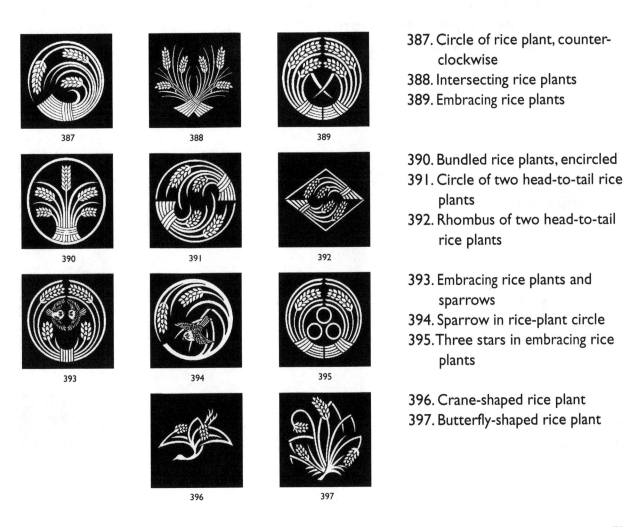

387. Circle of rice plant, counter-clockwise
388. Intersecting rice plants
389. Embracing rice plants

390. Bundled rice plants, encircled
391. Circle of two head-to-tail rice plants
392. Rhombus of two head-to-tail rice plants

393. Embracing rice plants and sparrows
394. Sparrow in rice-plant circle
395. Three stars in embracing rice plants

396. Crane-shaped rice plant
397. Butterfly-shaped rice plant

Ivy (*tsuta*)

A deciduous liana of the grape family, ivy was used in patterns and family crests because of its elegant beauty. In the Edo period, ivy crests were used by both the Matsudaira clan and the shōgun Tokugawa Yoshimune, so they became associated with power and authority. Geisha and prostitutes also loved to use these crests, but for quite a different reason. The way ivy twines around other plants and grows thick was said to symbolize the way these women depended upon their regular customers and never left them.

398. Ivy leaf, encircled
399. Ivy leaf in rice cake
400. Twisted ivy leaf

401. Pointed-leaf ivy
402. *Kōrin*-style shadowed ivy
403. Looped ivy

404. Pile of three ivy leaves
405. Three ivy leaves, encircled
406. Small ivy leaf, encircled

398

399

400

401

402

403

404

405

406

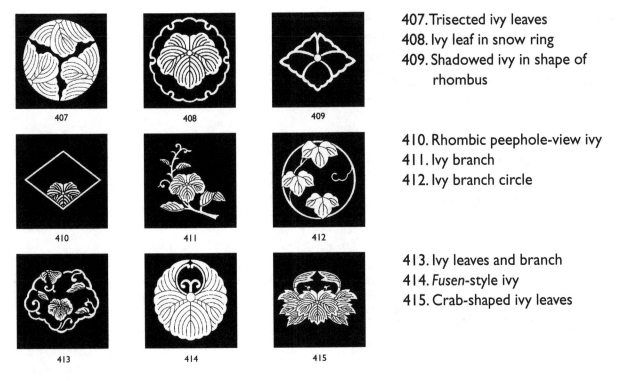

407. Trisected ivy leaves
408. Ivy leaf in snow ring
409. Shadowed ivy in shape of rhombus

410. Rhombic peephole-view ivy
411. Ivy branch
412. Ivy branch circle

413. Ivy leaves and branch
414. *Fusen*-style ivy
415. Crab-shaped ivy leaves

Clove (*chōji*)

An evergreen shrub of the potato family, the clove is native to Mexico. The crests depict the fruit of the clove plant, which was introduced to Japan in the beginning of the Heian period and appreciated for its medicinal and aromatic properties.

416. Encircled clove
417. Shadowed clove swirl, counterclockwise
418. Two clove swirls, clockwise

419. Three counterclockwise clove swirls, encircled
420. Trisected cloves
421. Intersecting cloves, encircled

 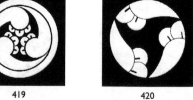 

419   420   421

422. Intersecting cloves
423. Three piled intersecting cloves
424. Three interlocking clove swirls

422   423   424

425. Four cloves and vines in shape of rhombus
426. Six cloves
427. Eight cloves, encircled

425   426   427

Ginkgo (*ichō*)

The Tokugawa clan was said to have used a crest depicting this deciduous tree's leaves before adopting the hollyhock.

428. Ginkgo leaf, encircled
429. Three ginkgo leaves
430. Three shadowed ginkgo leaves

428   429   430

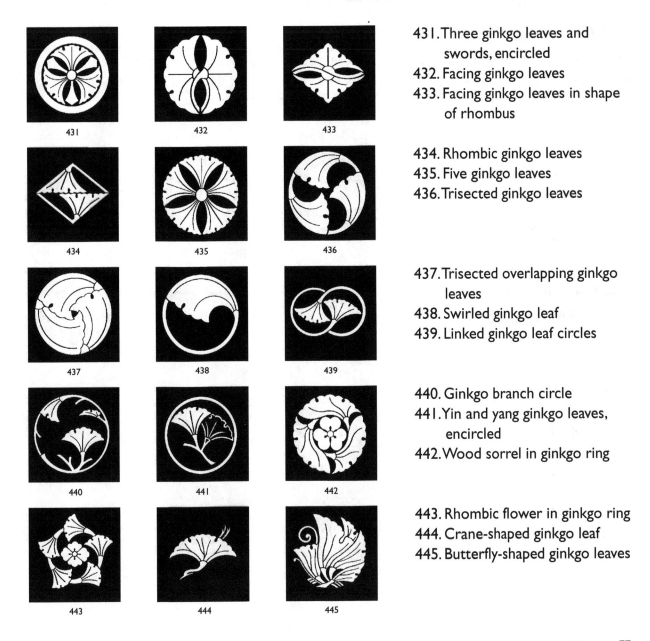

431. Three ginkgo leaves and swords, encircled
432. Facing ginkgo leaves
433. Facing ginkgo leaves in shape of rhombus

434. Rhombic ginkgo leaves
435. Five ginkgo leaves
436. Trisected ginkgo leaves

437. Trisected overlapping ginkgo leaves
438. Swirled ginkgo leaf
439. Linked ginkgo leaf circles

440. Ginkgo branch circle
441. Yin and yang ginkgo leaves, encircled
442. Wood sorrel in ginkgo ring

443. Rhombic flower in ginkgo ring
444. Crane-shaped ginkgo leaf
445. Butterfly-shaped ginkgo leaves

Iris (*kakitsubata*)

A perpetual plant, the iris has beautiful dark-purple flowers that bloom around May. Iris crests are known as the kamon of court nobles. Iris flowers were first depicted in patterns on the garments and palanquins of the nobility, and then later became family crests.

446. Iris bloom
447. Three iris blooms
448. Iris circle

449. Two irises
450. Circle of three irises
451. Embracing irises

452. Iris for the Nakayama family
453. Stem-to-stem irises in shape of rhombus
454. Standing iris

455. Looped iris
456. Crane-shaped iris

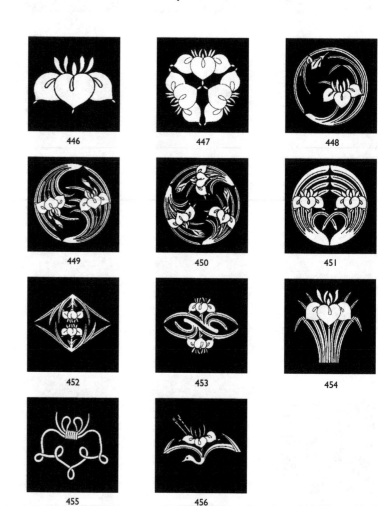

446

447

448

449

450

451

452

453

454

455

456

Cherry Blossom (*sakura*)

The cherry is a deciduous shrub or tree of the rose family. People enjoyed the elegant appearance of these trees and modeled crests after their beautiful blossoms. The Sakurai clan and the Yoshino clan adopted *sakura* kamon because of the association with their family names.

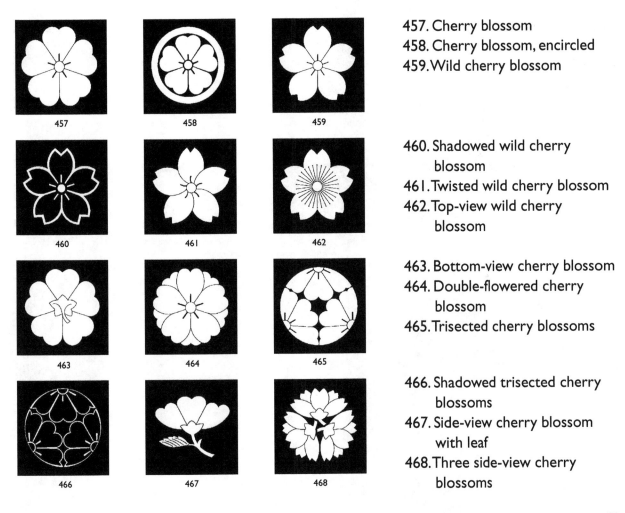

457. Cherry blossom
458. Cherry blossom, encircled
459. Wild cherry blossom

460. Shadowed wild cherry blossom
461. Twisted wild cherry blossom
462. Top-view wild cherry blossom

463. Bottom-view cherry blossom
464. Double-flowered cherry blossom
465. Trisected cherry blossoms

466. Shadowed trisected cherry blossoms
467. Side-view cherry blossom with leaf
468. Three side-view cherry blossoms

469. Cherry blossom branch
470. Circle of cherry blossom and branch
471. Circle of three cherry blossoms and leaves

472. Cherry blossom branch in disarray
473. Cherry blossom and embracing leaves
474. *Gyōyō*-style cherry blossom

475. *Fusen*-style cherry blossom
476. *Fusen*-style cherry blossom
477. Cherry blossom under crescent moon

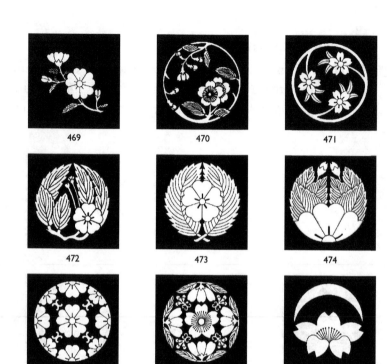

469

470

471

472

473

474

475

476

477

Animal Crests

Although there are fewer crests modeled after animals than plants, several major animal patterns exist, including those depicting mythological animals.

Lion and Peony (*shishi ni botan*)

The lion and peony combination has been used since the Heian period. The pattern seems to have originated from the belief that lions loved and ate peonies. The lion is a symbol of boldness and has been regarded as the king of beasts since ancient times, while peonies have been admired as noble, beautiful flowers. Since this pattern combines bravery and elegance, it was thought to embody the essence of the samurai, and was used to decorate armor and helmets.

478

479

478, 479. Peony and Chinese lion

Chinese Phoenix (*hō-ō*)

The phoenix, a mythological bird, was respected in China as one of the four spirits, along with *qilin* (a winged beast with one horn, a deer's body, a cow's tail, a horse's hooves, and a wolf's face), turtles, and dragons. It is said that the bird's appearance heralds the arrival of the holy king. This idea was introduced into Japan and the phoenix was often used in decorative patterns.

480

481

482

480. Phoenix circle
481. Circle of flying phoenix
482. Decorative phoenix for court celebrations

Crane (*tsuru*)

Since ancient times, cranes have been said to live for a thousand years, so they have been considered omens of longevity. According to legend, there was a Japanese crane of great beauty that flew with a hermit on its back.

Crane motifs became quite popular, especially in the Kamakura period, and when the Kamakura shogunate dedicated swords to the shrine of each region in Japan, they were decorated with the pattern of a crane in a circle (*tsuru-maru*). Later, the crane pattern became widely used for family crests.

483. Crane circle
484. Circle of *Kōrin*-style crane
485. Facing cranes

486. Facing cranes in shape of rhombus
487. *Kōrin*-style cranes in shape of bellflower
488. Standing crane in tortoiseshell
489. Dancing crane in flight
490. Paper crane

483

484

485

486

487

488

489

490

Turtle (*kame*)

The model for turtle kamon is a kind of turtle design called *minogame*, in which the turtle has seaweed trailing behind it, making it appear as if wearing a *mino* (straw raincoat). The turtle is also drawn with ears, which the real animal does not have. Like cranes, turtles were regarded as a symbol of long life. Before becoming family crests, turtle patterns were used for various decorative purposes in the Fujiwara period (897–1185).

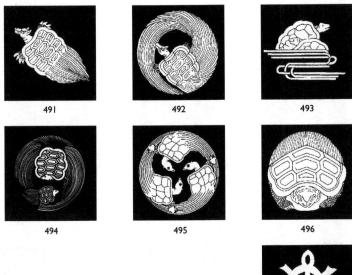

491. Single turtle
492. Turtle circle
493. Turtle and water

494. Turtle with child
495. Three head-to-tail turtles
496. Head-on turtle

497. Disordered character turtle

Dragon (*ryū*)

The dragon is another mythical beast, often referred to as king of the scaled animals. This monstrous creature was thought to have supernatural powers, like the phoenix. The pattern was used not only for clothes and swords, but also to decorate palaces, shrines, and temples in the Kamakura and Muromachi periods. Samurai warriors were especially partial to dragon kamon.

498. Dragon circle
499. Dragon circle
500. Rain dragon

498

499

500

501. Three rain dragons
502. Intersecting dragon talons

501

502

Hawk (*taka*), Hawk Feathers (*takano-ha*)

Because of their bold, predatory nature, hawks were a symbol of war and fighting spirit, therefore, it was common for military commanders to adopt these kamon. High-level members of the ancient Imperial Guard were known to use hawk feathers on their elaborate ceremonial crowns.

503. Hawk circle
504. Facing hawks
505. Intersecting hawk feathers

503

504

505

506

507

508

506. Two parallel hawk feathers, encircled
507. Wheel of hawk feathers
508. Circle of hawk feather

509

510

511

509. Nail puller (*kugi-nuki*) in circle of facing hawk feathers
510. Fan of hawk feathers
511. Butterfly-shaped hawk feathers

Wild Goose (*kari*)

Wild geese arrive in large flocks in southern regions during the autumn months, and following their migratory instincts, head back north in spring. The Japanese have written poems and songs expressing an affinity for wild geese since ancient times. In the Fujiwara period, the bird was depicted in various decorative patterns; later it was turned into a kamon motif.

512

513

514

512. Wild goose
513. Looped wild goose, encircled
514. Three looped wild geese, heads facing outward

515

516

517

515. Three wild geese inward-facing, encircled
516. Interlocking wild geese
517. Wild-geese wheel

518. Wild geese in shape of
 rhombus
519. Peephole-view wild goose in
 rhombus
520. Flying wild goose

518   519   520

521. Three flying wild geese

521

Dove (*hato*)

Doves were referred to as sacred animals of Hachiman, a Bodhisattva worshiped as a god of war. It was said that if military commanders wrote the name of the Bodhisattva on their banners, doves would flock to their camp. Thus, it became common for military leaders to adopt dove patterns as their kamon. In these crests, doves are often combined with other motifs, such as *hoya* (mistletoe) and *torii*.

522. Dove
523. Facing doves
524. Facing doves in flight

522   523   524

525. Dove with children
526. Facing doves and *torii*
527. Dove circle

525   526   527

Rabbit (*usagi*)

Rabbits, like cranes and turtles, have long been considered lucky animals. Their crests were probably chosen for auspicious symbolism.

528

529

530

528. Head-on rabbit
529. Three back-view rabbits
530. Three rabbits

531

531. Rabbit and waves

Butterfly (*chō*)

Butterflies have been used in patterns since the Nara period. These designs were used not only for clothes and furnishings but also for armor, helmets, and other battle gear. Both samurai and court nobles loved butterfly designs.

532

533

534

532. Encircled butterfly
533. Facing butterflies
534. Three butterflies

535. Shadowed *Kōrin*-style
butterfly
536. Three flying butterflies
537. Circle of three butterflies

535

536

537

538. Butterfly wheel
539. Peephole-view butterfly,
encircled
540. *Fusen*-style butterfly

538

539

540

541. Facing butterflies and three
swirls
542. Three butterflies and *mokkō*
543. Butterfly-shaped looped vine

541

542

543

Dragonfly (*tonbo*)

Emperor Yūryaku was once bitten on the elbow by a horsefly, soon after which the horsefly was captured by a dragonfly. His admiration of this scene was so great that he composed a poem about it, and the poem was included in the *Nihon Shoki* (Chronicle of Japan). Thereafter, samurai came to refer to dragonflies as *kachi-mushi* (victorious insect); they were often used as decorations for quivers and other battle gear.

544. Three dragonflies

544

Tool and Implement Crests

These kamon depict everyday items of ancient Japan.

Prayer Rod (*nusa* or *hei*)

These wooden rods with long strands of paper trailing from them were used in Shintō deification ritual, and thus were respected as sacred tools. Samurai believed that spirits dwelled in the rods, so they invoked the help and protection of the gods by using prayer-rod designs as their kamon. Some Shintō priests also used these kamon because of their religious symbolism.

Prayer rod (right) and
earthenware pot (left)

545

545. Prayer rod

546

547

548

546. Prayer rod, encircled
547. Crossed prayer rod
548. Three prayer rods

Tray (*oshiki*)

In ancient times, people folded up the edges of leaves to make tray-like platters. Over time, the bark of the *hinoki* (Japanese cypress) was used instead of leaves. *Oshiki* were mainly used to offer food to the gods, so these crests were adopted for religious reasons. *Oshiki* crests depict the tray as seen from above, usually with some object or kanji character on it, probably to emphasize its function as an offering tray.

549. Tray
550. Well frame on tray
551. Ivy on tray

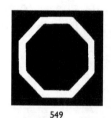
549

550

551

Oshiki

Earthenware Pot (*heishi*)

Special bottles used to offer sake to the gods were considered holy vessels. Shintō priests and their relatives often used them as kamon designs.

552. Earthenware pot
553. Parallel earthenware pots
554. Shrine earthenware pots, encircled

555. Trisected earthenware pots
556. Five earthenware pots
557. Earthenware pot on tray

Cross (*kurusu*)

The Japanese word for this Christian symbol is from the Portuguese, *cruz*. Christian converts originally adopted these crests to express their religious beliefs. However, after the Tokugawa shogunate banned the religion, most Christians hid their faith and adopted different kamon designs. Consequently, most cross designs have disappeared.

558. Cross
559. Cut-bamboo cross
560. Flower cross

Gion Talisman (Gion *mamori*)

These crests were modeled after the religious charm of the Gion Shrine, where Gozu Tennō (a guardian deity) was worshiped. Originally, people who worshiped at the Gion Shrine adopted these crests. Later, Christians used the crests as a disguised symbol of the cross.

561. Gion talisman, encircled
562. Cylindrical Gion talisman
563. Talisman for the Ikeda family

561

562

563

Dharma Chakra (*rinpō*)

Ancient Indians worshiped the *rinpō*, a legendary weapon. According to legend, it is one of the weapons of the emperor Tenrin Jō-ō (Chakravartin). When he turns the wheel of the *rinpō* in the battlefield, it smooths out uneven ground, removes obstacles, and brings peace and happiness to the world. It is also one of the symbols used in Esoteric Buddhism.

564. Dharma Chakra
565. Rhombic Dharma Chakra
566. Trisected Dharma Chakra

564

565

566

Bow and Arrow (*yumi-ya*)

The bow and arrow was used both for hunting and as a weapon of war. It seems to have been adopted into kamon designs because it symbolized the samurai spirit, although it was also used in non-martial ceremonies and rituals.

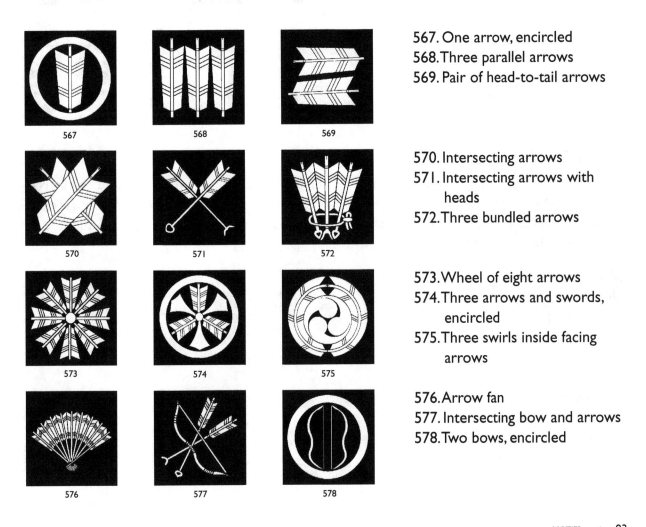

567. One arrow, encircled
568. Three parallel arrows
569. Pair of head-to-tail arrows

570. Intersecting arrows
571. Intersecting arrows with heads
572. Three bundled arrows

573. Wheel of eight arrows
574. Three arrows and swords, encircled
575. Three swirls inside facing arrows

576. Arrow fan
577. Intersecting bow and arrows
578. Two bows, encircled

579. Five bows
580. Four bows in shape of
     rhombus
581. Arrow nock

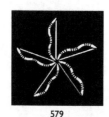  

579   580   581

582. Folded arrow nock
583. Three overlapping arrow
     nocks
584. Three arrow nocks and swords

582   583   584

Snake Eye (*janome*)

These kamon were originally modeled after *tsurumaki*, a leather, ring-shaped spool used to reel bowstring. The *tsurumaki* was an essential part of a samurai's battle gear. Later, the design came to be called *janome* simply because of its resemblance to a snake's eye. It was usually adopted by samurai families for its warrior symbolism.

585. Snake eye
586. Yin and yang snake eyes
587. Four snake eyes

585   586   587

588. Seven snake eyes
589. Trisected snake eyes,
     encircled
590. Three snake eyes and swords

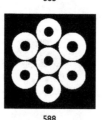  

588   589   590

Apricot-Leaf Harness Accessory (*gyōyō*)

Gyōyō was a harness accessory made either of metal or leather, originally introduced from China. It apparently got its name from its shape, which resembles an apricot leaf. As a horse galloped, the *gyōyō* was considered a beautiful sight as it fluttered in the wind. These crests are often confused with *myōga* crests because of their similarity in shape.

In the Ashikaga period (1333–1568), samurai often adopted *gyōyō* crests. The Ōtomo clan in Kyushu greatly expanded their territory after adopting the crest, so *gyōyō* crests became the envy of all the generals in Kyushu. They envied it so much that when a general was victorious, he would steal the enemy's *gyōyō* crests, which would then be taken by another general in the same way.

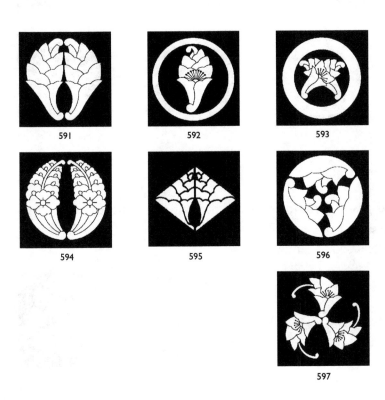

591. Embracing *gyōyō*
592. Encircled *gyōyō*
593. Intersecting *gyōyō*, encircled

594. Embracing *gyōyō* with rhombic flowers
595. Embracing *gyōyō* in shape of rhombus
596. Trisected *gyōyō*

597. Swirled *gyōyō* with blossoms

Bit (*kutsuwa*)

Kutsuwa is supposedly a dialectal variation of *kuchiwa* (muzzle). The bit is an iron fitting which is inserted into a horse's mouth to fasten the reins. The ends of the bit are circular, and it is these circles that were depicted. These crests were mostly used to symbolize martial spirit, but Christians seeking to covertly display their faith also adopted the cross-like patterns.

598. Bit
599. Flower bit
600. Snow-covered bit

598

599

600

601. Square bit
602. Rhombic bit
603. Three connected bits

601

602

603

Genji Cart (*Genji-guruma*)

The Genji cart, or oxcart, also called *gosho guruma* (cart for the Imperial Palace), was often symbolized by depicting only the wheel of the cart. After the Fujiwara period, the wheel was depicted in decorative patterns and later used as family crests.

604. Genji cart
605. Flowered Genji carts,
     overlapping
606. Japanese pinwheel

604

605

606

Round Fan (*uchiwa*)

The round fan is made by covering bamboo ribs with rice paper, and is still used in modern Japan to cool off during the summer. Both court nobles and commoners have used these patterns through the years, but the reason it became a family crest is uncertain.

607

608

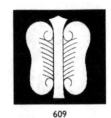

609

607. Round fan, encircled
608. Three round fans
609. Chinese fan

610

610. Three Chinese fans

Feather Fan (*ha-uchiwa*)

Fans made from feathers are said to be a distinctive possession of the *tengu*, a magical long-nosed goblin of Japanese folklore. These designs have been used for shrine crests and temple crests.

611

612

611. Feather fan
612. Trisected feather fans

Military Leader's Fan (*gunbai uchiwa*)

Military leaders in the Sengoku period used this special fan when commanding their armies. It was usually made of leather and iron. In the Battle of Kawanakajima, Uesugi Kenshin attacked Takeda Shingen with his sword, but Shingen is said to have protected himself with this fan. Using this crest seems to have symbolized faith in the war god Marishiten.

613. Military leader's fan

613

Fan (*ōgi*)

When a fan is opened, it spreads out from a single point, symbolizing the way life develops. Because of this association, the fan is used in ceremonies as an auspicious object, expressing a celebration of life. Also, because of its elegant form, fan patterns were often depicted in picture scrolls from the Fujiwara period to the Kamakura period.

614. Rising sun on fan
615. Cherry blossom on fan
616. Layered fans

614

615

616

617. Three fans, encircled
618. Pile of three fans
619. Five interlaced fans

617

618

619

620

621

622

620. Two parallel fans, encircled
621. Intersecting fans, encircled
622. Fans in shape of well frame

623

624

625

623. Japanese cypress fan
624. Rhombic fans
625. Butterfly-shaped fans

Sandbank (*suhama*)

The sandbank kamon depicts a pattern in the shape of a sandbank, which represents a certain holy place on Mount Hōrai. In the Fujiwara period, these patterns were used as celebratory decorations, so the motif was used on clothes and furnishings as a pattern of good fortune.

626

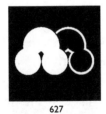

627

628

626. Sandbank
627. Yin and yang sandbanks
628. Intersecting sandbanks

629

630

631

629. Three sandbanks
    inward-facing
630. Kōrin-style sandbank
631. Trisected sandbanks

632. Flower-shaped sandbank
633. Three sandbanks and vines,
    encircled

632

633

Nail Puller (*kugi-nuki*)

The *kugi-nuki* kamon depicts an ancient carpenter's tool that was used to pull nails. It consisted of a square metal washer and a lever. The lever was put into the hole of the washer, and the nail was pulled out. *Kugi-nuki* were also called *kuki wo nuku*, an ambiguous phrase which could be taken to mean either "pull nails" or "capture nine castles." It is thought that because of this alternate meaning, the kamon was adopted as an omen of victory.

634. Nail puller
635. Linked nail pullers, encircled
636. Nail puller, encircled

634

635

636

Rice Cake (*mochi*)

Sticky rice is steamed and pounded to make the Japanese rice cake, used for both Shintō and Buddhist ceremonies since ancient times. Crest designs include both *kuro-mochi* (black rice cake) and *shiro-mochi* (white rice cake). The kanji for *kuro-mochi* can also be read *koku-mochi*, which means "military leader's raise in income," so this kamon was used in the hope of bringing good fortune.

637. Black rice cake
638. Rhombic rice cake

637

638

Coin (*zeni* or *sen*)

Some coins depicted in kamon are inscribed with kanji characters. *Kan'eitsūhō* (of Japanese origin), *seiwatsūhō*, and *eirakutsūhō* (both of Chinese origin) are common examples of kanji coins. Because the characters on these coins signified good luck, it is likely that they were used as crest motifs for their auspicious symbolism.

Blank coins were usually arranged in a pattern of one to six coins on a crest, although sometimes as many as nine were shown. Kamon depicting more than six coins are called *rensen* (a series of coins). These designs seem to have been chosen for their religious meaning.

Rokurensen is a special design in which six blank coins are arranged in two rows of three. This pattern represents *rokudō*, the six worlds of Buddhism. These include hell, the world of starvation, the world of animality, the world of constant war, the human world, and the world of joy. After death, it is thought that the deceased will journey into the next world, and six coins are put into the coffin as fare for crossing the Sanzu River (comparable to the River Styx in Greek mythology). The coins may also have been adopted as a kamon design in the hope that Jizōson, or Ksitigarbha, would save all beings in all the six worlds.

639

640

641

639. *Eiraku* coin
640. Wave coin
641. Six coins for the Sanada family

Weight (*fundō*)

Weight motifs depict the weights that were used on old-fashioned scales. Though the reason why the motif was adopted as a family crest is uncertain, one opinion holds that it was because of a weight's fanciful design and ability to measure weight accurately.

642. Weight
643. Weight in rhombus
644. Yin and yang weights

642

643

644

645. Three weights
646. Weights in shape of cherry blossom

645

646

Wooden Measure (*masu*)

Masu is the name of a wooden measure, but it is also a homophone that means "to increase," so this design was thought to bring good fortune.

647. Wooden measure
648. Three nested wooden measures, encircled
649. Pile of three wooden measures

647

648

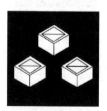
649

Others

Other everyday items that were adapted into kamon include the traditional gift decoration (*noshi*), ship (*fune*), sail (*ho*), paddle (*kai*), helmet ornament (*kuwagata*), sword (*ken*), *aka-tori* (tool used to remove dirt from a comb), umbrella (*kasa*), sedge hat (*kasa*), and sickle (*kama*).

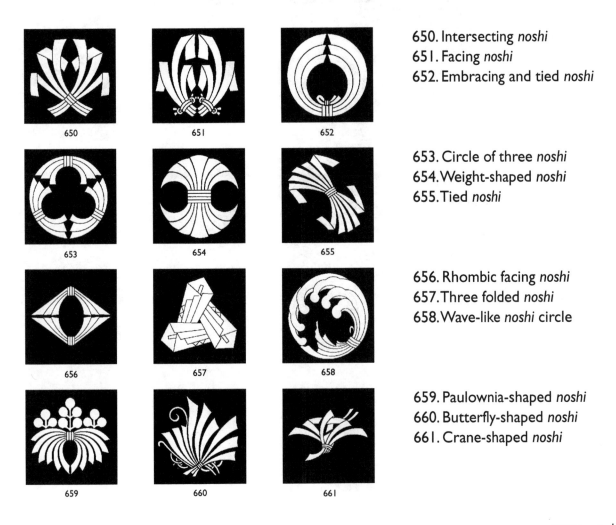

650. Intersecting *noshi*
651. Facing *noshi*
652. Embracing and tied *noshi*

653. Circle of three *noshi*
654. Weight-shaped *noshi*
655. Tied *noshi*

656. Rhombic facing *noshi*
657. Three folded *noshi*
658. Wave-like *noshi* circle

659. Paulownia-shaped *noshi*
660. Butterfly-shaped *noshi*
661. Crane-shaped *noshi*

662. Sailboat
663. Treasure boat and waves

662

663

664. Encircled sail
665. Sail and mist
666. Circle of five sails

664

665

666

667. Intersecting paddles,
      encircled
668. Three intersecting paddles

667

668

669. Samurai helmet, encircled

669

670. Three swords
671. Eight swords in shape of
      rhombus

670

671

672. Helmet ornament with star

673. Intersecting sickles, encircled

674, 675. *Aka-tori*

674

675

676. Single umbrella

676

677. Three-tiered sedge hat

677

Construction Crests

Torii

It is thought that *torii*, the famous Shintō shrine gates, originated from the perches on which sacrificial chickens for the gods sat. *Torii* crests were chosen for their religious symbolism.

678. *Torii*
679. *Torii* and Japanese cedars

678

679

Flagstone (*ishi-datami*)

Flagstone crests were modeled after various arrangements of square flagstones used to pave the ground. The checkerboard-like designs were first used as decorative patterns, and then evolved into crests.

680. Four flagstones
681. Encircled flagstones

680

681

Well Frame (*i-zutsu, i-geta*)

The square frame gives Japanese wells their distinctive appearance. It was quite common for people with the kanji for *i* (well) in their family names to use these crests.

682. Well frame
683. Folded well frame, encircled
684. Yin and yang overlapping well frames

685. Three swirls in well frame
686. Rhombic well frame
687. Linked well frames

688. Three well frames
689. *Mokkō* in well frame

Pattern Crests

Although some pattern crests depicted real objects, most were used for their aesthetic shape and geometrical design.

Swirl (*tomoe*)

There are various views about the origin of the swirl design. One holds that it was originally modeled after a *tomo*, a leather elbow pad used by archers long ago to protect skin from chafing against the bowstring. Another opinion holds that it was based on a comma-shaped bead, which was a symbol of family prosperity, while still another conjecture holds that the pattern may have been introduced from China.

Because of its resemblance to swirling water, the *tomoe* design became a symbol for water. As a result, it was placed on the roof tiles and gables of houses and temples as a charm to ward off fire. *Tomoe* is the kamon of Hachiman, the war god, so it was also used as a divine crest in shrines throughout Japan.

690. Single counterclockwise swirl
691. Three clockwise swirls
692. Three clockwise swirls in
    rhombus

690

691

692

693. Three swirls in shape of
    square
694. Three long-tailed swirls
695. Three big and small swirls,
    clockwise

693

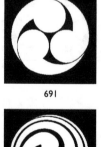
694

695

696. Yin and yang *magatama* (fang-shaped accessories), swirled
697. Intersecting swirls, encircled
698. Two linked swirls

699. Three looped swirls
700. Five interlocking swirls
701. Twisted swirls

702. Swirls in shape of ball
703. Whirlpool
704. Pile of three single swirls

705. Seven swirls
706. Kanji character for *tomoe* (swirl), encircled
707. Circle of three *tomoe* characters

Rhombus (*hishi*)

The symbolic meaning of the rhombus is uncertain, but it has been common in decorative patterns since the Nara period and appears very frequently in kamon designs.

708. Shadowed rhombus
709. Thin and thick rhombus
710. Two-tiered rhombuses

711. Three-tiered rhombuses, encircled
712. Rhombic pine bark
713. Divided rhombus

714. Four rhombic flowers
715. Linked rhombuses
716. Four layered rhombuses, encircled

717. Three rhombuses, encircled
718. Bellflower-shaped rhombuses
719. Three three-tiered rhombuses

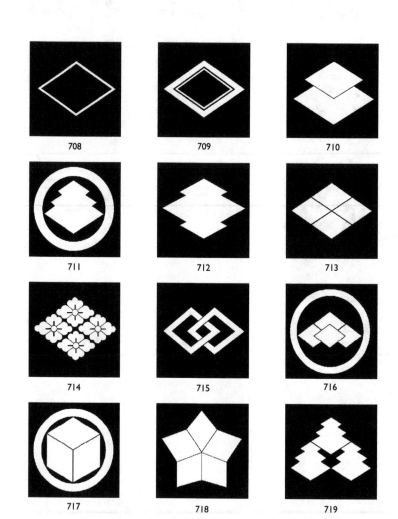

Line (*hikiryō*)

There are various views on the origin of encircled lines or bars. The word *hikiryō* can be written several different ways in Japanese, so its meaning is ambiguous. It may simply mean "two parallel lines," which is a straightforward geometrical description of the pattern. Another possible origin of the design is the encampment curtains used long ago by samurai families. These curtains consisted of five pieces of cloth dyed different colors such as black and dark blue that were sewn together horizontally. A different combination of colors represented each family. Yet a third view holds that because the *ryō* of *hikiryō* also means "spirit" or "dragon," the design was a superstitious or religious symbol of some kind.

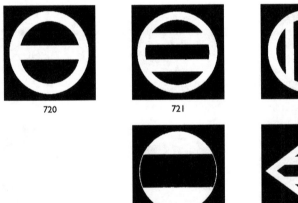

720

721

722

723

724

720. Single line, encircled
721. Two lines, encircled
722. Three vertical lines, encircled

723. Single line for the Nitta family
724. Two lines in rhombus

Japanese Quince (*mokkō*)

Although the name of this pattern is *mokkō* (Japanese quince, a small tree of the rose family), its origin is unclear. It may at one time have had some relationship to the Japanese quince itself, but there is another theory that it symbolized the cross-section cut of a cucumber. A third view holds that it was a pattern used to decorate *sudare* (bamboo blinds) that were imported from China in ancient times. Whatever the case, these patterns have been used as decorations for oxcarts, palanquins, and clothing since ancient times, and eventually came to be used in kamon as well.

725. *Mokkō*
726. Pile of three *mokkō*
727. Bisected *mokkō*

728. *Mokkō* in rhombus
729. Peephole-view *mokkō*, encircled
730. *Mokkō* and vines

731. Wood sorrel in *mokkō*
732. Three swirls in shadowed *mokkō*
733. *Mokkō*-shaped swirl

725   726   727
728   729   730
731   732   733

734

735

736

734. Intersecting hawk feathers in *mokkō*
735. *Mokkō* in rice cake
736. *Mokkō* under mountain shape

737

737. *Mokkō* in hut

Square-eyes (*meyui*)

The *meyui* pattern is made of squares with small dots in the center that look like eyes. It was popular in the Kamakura period, and later came to be used in family crests.

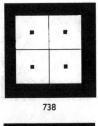

738

739

740

738. Four-square-eyes
739. Tilted four-square-eyes, encircled
740. Three-square-eyes, encircled

741

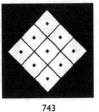

742

743

741. Shadowed rhombic four-square-eyes
742. Small four-square-eyes in threadlike circle
743. Nine-square-eyes

744. Layered five-square-eyes
745. Looped four-square-eyes
746. Three rhombic
     four-square-eyes

744   745   746

747. Twisted four-square-eyes
748. Wheel of four-square-eyes
749. Four-square-eyes and swords

747   748   749

Chain-Linked Circles (*wachigai*)

The simple *wachigai* pattern depicts two or more circles connected like a chain. *Wachigai* seems to have been adopted as a family crest design because the elegant pattern was used prevalently in the Fujiwara period.

750. Linked circles
751. Linked circles in rice cake
752. Linked circle and square

750   751   752

753. Three interlocking circles,
     encircled
754. Four interlocking circles
755. Looped interlocking circles

753   754   755

  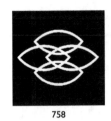

756 757 758

756. Interlocking circles and flower circle
757. Six interlocking circles
758. *Mokkō*-shaped interlocking circles

Scales (*uroko*)

The scale design was made famous by the Hōjō clan. According to the *Taiheiki* (Chronicle of the Great Peace), when Hōjō Tokimasa went to Enoshima Benzaiten to pray, a beautiful woman appeared, turned into a giant snake, and disappeared into the sea. The snake left behind three big scales, so he modeled his kamon after the scales to commemorate the event.

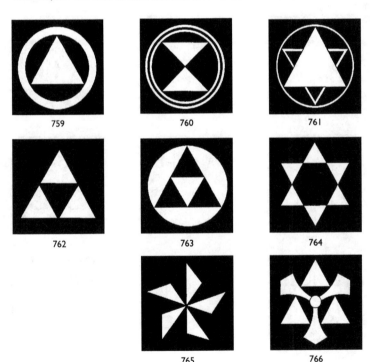

759 760 761

762 763 764

765 766

759. Encircled scale
760. Facing scales in double circle
761. Yin and yang layered scales, encircled

762. Three scales
763. Three scales in rice cake
764. Six scales

765. Wheel of five scales
766. Three scales and swords

Tortoiseshell (*kikkō*)

Hexagonal patterns like those shown below were modeled after the shell of a tortoise. They were especially popular as family crests in the Heian period because of their well-proportioned, attractive hexagonal shape, and because tortoises were considered auspicious animals.

767. Tortoiseshell
768. Linked tortoiseshells
769. Three intersecting tortoise-
      shells

770. Square flower in tortoiseshell
771. Three oak leaves in
      tortoiseshell
772. Two arrows in tortoiseshell

773. Trisected tortoiseshells and
      rhombic flowers
774. Pile of three tortoiseshells
775. Pile of three tortoiseshells
      and rhombic flowers

776. *Bishamon*-style tortoiseshells
777. Flower in tortoiseshell
778. Tortoiseshell in disarray

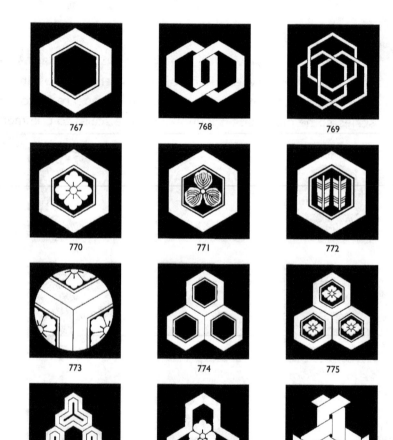

767   768   769

770   771   772

773   774   775

776   777   778

Chinese Flower (*karahana*)

The Chinese flower motif is not patterned after a specific plant. Rather, it is simply a flower drawn in the Chinese style. The design was introduced from the Asian continent and became quite common during the Heian period.

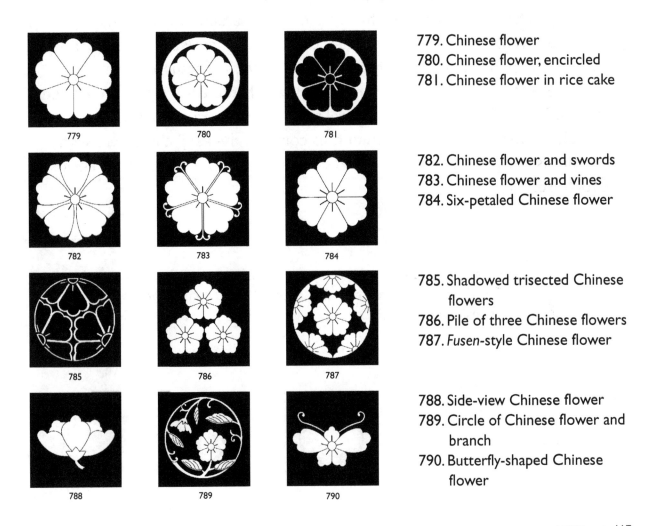

779. Chinese flower
780. Chinese flower, encircled
781. Chinese flower in rice cake

782. Chinese flower and swords
783. Chinese flower and vines
784. Six-petaled Chinese flower

785. Shadowed trisected Chinese flowers
786. Pile of three Chinese flowers
787. *Fusen*-style Chinese flower

788. Side-view Chinese flower
789. Circle of Chinese flower and branch
790. Butterfly-shaped Chinese flower

Kanji Character Crests

Characters were used in crests because of the characters' meaning, historical background, or both. Many of them symbolize luck, prosperity, or religious belief, and some commemorate special events or people.

Although a few kamon portray the syllabic *kana* characters, most are kanji (Chinese-derived) characters. Basic character fonts include: *kakuji-gata*, block style; *kaisho*, regular brush-stroke style; *gyōsho*, semi-cursive; and *sōsho*, cursive.

In addition to these basic fonts, various stylized characters were also depicted in kamon. Some of these kept the original form of the character, while others were quite abstract. It was also common to combine the kanji characters with other motifs and patterns, such as in *kikkō ni yūnoji* (kanji for "existence" enclosed in a tortoiseshell).

一 (*ichi*, one)

The kanji numeral one symbolized being the first to arrive at the battlefield, and may have also represented a spearhead. The character can also be read *katsu*, which means "to win." For these reasons, it was considered symbolic of the samurai spirit.

791. Kanji numeral *ichi*, encircled
792. Kanji characters for *ichi-ban* (the first)

791   792

八 (*hachi*, eight)

The numeral eight was appreciated because its shape broadens toward the bottom, symbolizing eternal expansion. Also, it is the initial character of Hachiman, a war god. These seem to be the main reasons why this character was used for family crests.

793

794

793. Kanji numeral *hachi*
794. Kanji numeral *hachi*, encircled

十 (*jū*, ten)

The origin of kamon depicting the numeral ten is unclear. One theory is that it was a modification of *hikiryō*, another claims that the two lines symbolize two dragons, and yet a third view holds that it was used to represent the Christian cross. None of these theories, however, is widely accepted. The Shimazu clan is well known for this kamon.

795

795. Kanji numeral *jū*, encircled

卍 (*manji*, swastika)

This Buddhist symbol was initially introduced from India, and it became widely associated with temples in Japan. Called *svastika* in Sanskrit, it is a lucky omen which appears on Buddha's chest and the soles of his feet, where good fortune and virtue gather. The symbol has appeared in many places throughout history, such as ancient Babylon, Assyria, Greece, and the Roman Empire. It is unclear whether these swastikas had a single common origin, but they seem to have often represented the sun. In Japan, the mark was and is widely used as a symbol of Buddhism and Buddhist temples, and was adopted as a family crest in the hope of receiving good fortune.

796. Clockwise swastika
797. Swastika in rice cake
798. Swords in shape of swastika

799. Stylized swastika
800. Rhombic swastika
801. Tilted swastika in disarray

802. Five swastikas
803. Circular swastika
804. Twisted swastika

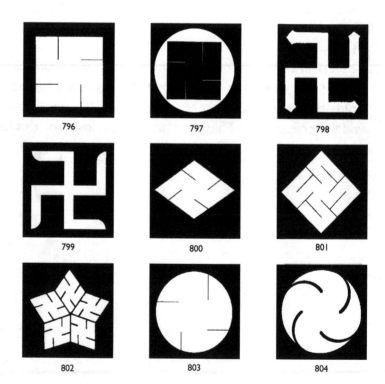

大 (*dai*, big)

The *dai* character connotes development and growth; therefore, it was adopted as a kamon in hopes of bringing success and fortune to the family. Families who have the character in their surnames also used these crests.

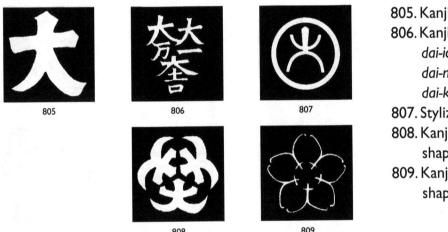

805. Kanji character for *dai*
806. Kanji characters for:
     dai-ichi (big one),
     dai-man (big ten thousand),
     dai-kichi (big fortune)
807. Stylized kanji for *dai*, encircled
808. Kanji characters for *dai* in shape of wood sorrel
809. Kanji characters for *dai* in shape of cherry blossom

無 (*mu*, nothing)

The character 無 expresses the basic principles of Zen Buddhism. Zen philosophers frequently mention it as a straightforward expression of fundamental Zen concepts such as *shogyō mujō* (all things are in flux, nothing is permanent) and *issai kaikū* (all of existence is unsubstantial and empty). Therefore, it is likely that Zen practitioners adopted crests bearing this character.

810, 811. Kanji character for *mu*, encircled

Others

Other characters commonly found in crests are 吉 (*kichi*, good luck), 加 (*ka*, add) 丸 (*maru*, circle), 上 (*ue*, top), 寿 (*kotobuki*, happiness), 福 (*fuku*, fortune), 鶴 (*tsuru*, crane), and 亀 (*kame*, turtle).

812. Kanji character for *kichi*
813. Kanji character for *ka*
814. Kanji character for *maru*

812

813

814

815. Kanji character for *jō*, encircled
816. Kanji character for *kotobuki*, encircled
817. Kanji character for *fuku*, encircled
818. Kanji character for *tsuru*, encircled
819. Kanji character for *kame*, encircled

815

816

817

818

819

Diagram and Charm Crests

Some crests originated from diagrams or charms. The designs of these kamon are neither characters nor patterns.

Kuji Mantra

The nine lines of this grid-like design symbolize the nine characters of the *Kuji* Mantra. *Kuji* consists of " 臨兵闘者皆陣列在前 ." This sacred incantation was derived from *Bao-pu Zi*, an ancient Chinese book that explained the ideas of Taoism. It is said that you can escape from disaster by chanting the mantra while drawing four vertical lines and five horizontal lines in the air. Not only Taoists, but also Buddhists of the Shingon sect and mountain ascetics were known to recite this mantra. The *kuji* design, therefore, seems to have been adopted for religious reasons.

820

820. *Kuji* symbol, encircled

Genji Incense Diagram (*Genjikō-zu*)

The Genji incense diagram shows the symbols used in *Genjikō*, an incense guessing game. *Kō* (incense) is said to have first been used for mortuary tablet purification rituals in India and China, and it was introduced to Japan by the sixth century. It became a popular item among the rich noble class around the eighth century. In addition to its use in religious rituals, incense was also burned to scent rooms and clothes.

Kumikō, a game where the object was to match and guess scents correctly, was fashionable in Japan at one time. The host burned incense combinations, and the guests were to guess what scents they were. *Genjikō* was one particular version of the game. In it, guests used fifty-two symbols named after the fifty-four chapters of *Genji Monogatari* (The Tale of Genji, a famous novel written by Murasaki Shikibu during the Heian period). Of the fifty-two symbols, only *hana-chiru-sato* and *hatsu-ne* were used as family crest motifs. Though the reason why they were used for family crests is unclear, it is probably because the forms were elegant.

821. *Hana-chiru-sato*
822. *Hatsu-ne*

821   822

VIII. God Crests

Just as families use crests, so too do shrines. Their crests are known as "god crests." These crests symbolize the different shrines, and much can be learned about the origin and history of each shrine by studying its crest.

823

824

823. Kasuga Shrine (Nara): *sagari fuji* (hanging wisteria)
824. Fushimi Inari Shrine (Kyoto): *ine* (rice plant)

825

825. Tsurugaoka Hachiman Shrine (Kanagawa): *tsuru* (crane)
826. Hie Shrine (Tokyo): *aoi* (hollyhock)

Storehouse of Hie Shrine

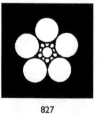

827

828

829

830

827. Yushima Shrine (Tokyo): *umebachi* (*umebachi*-style plum blossom)
828. Kumano Shrine (Wakayama): *karasu* (crow)

829. Izumo Shrine (Shimane): *kikkō ni ken hanabishi* (swords and rhombic flower in tortoiseshell)
830. Kotohira Shrine (Kagawa): *maru kon* (kanji character for *kon*, encircled)

Wall of Yushima Shrine

Gable of Yushima Shrine

IX. TEMPLE CRESTS

Temples also have crests. Some temples adopted the crests that their founders had used before they renounced the world, others were based on the doctrines of the various sects, and still others were modeled after the religious implements used by ascetics.

In addition, authorities such as the Imperial Household and the shogunate sometimes bestowed their crests upon certain temples. Powerful clans and feudal lords also had their family crests put on the buildings and utensils of temples to exhibit the families' power and influence.

831. Kongōbuji temple (Wakayama): *kiri* (paulownia)
832. Kenchōji temple (Kanagawa): *uroko* (scales)

831

832

Roof of Kenchōji temple

833. Zōjōji temple (Tokyo): *aoi* (hollyhock)
834. Enryakuji temple (Shiga): *kikurinpō* (Dharma Chakra at center of chrysanthemum)

833

834

Incense burner of Zōjōji temple

Zōjōji temple

X. Entertainment Crests

In the entertainment world of old Japan, various schools competed for influence and prestige within any given field of art. Entertainers usually took on the kamon of their school's master to promote the school's reputation of tradition and artful mastery. When a student of a certain school became established and well known, he would create his own identity or style of performance by combining his teacher's crest with his own. This identified him independently and also gave credit to his teacher. Sometimes when an actor became popular, his crest became the latest fashion around Edo (Tokyo).

Kabuki and Nō actors, Nō farce entertainers, and traditional dancers all had their own crests. The examples listed below show the crests of Kabuki actors.

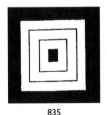
835

836

835. Ichikawa Danjūrō: *mitsumasu* (three wooden measures)
836. Nakamura Kichiemon: *ageha no chō* (butterfly)

837. Ichikawa Ennosuke: *mitsuzaru* (three monkeys)
838. Onoe Kikugorō: *kasane ōgi ni daki kashiwa*
(embracing oak leaves on layered fans)

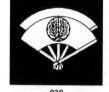

837

838

839. Sawamura Sōjūrō: *maruni inoji* (*hiragana* character
for *i*, encircled)
840. Kataoka Nizaemon: *maruni futatsu biki* (two lines
encircled)

839

840

XI. Crests of the Sengoku-Period Generals

Mōri Motonari (1497–1571)

Motonari was a famous *daimyō* who ruled ten provinces in the Chūgoku region. There is a very famous story about the time Motonari advised his three children, saying, "One arrow breaks easily, but if three arrows are bound together and become one, they will never break. In the same way, the three of you should cooperate with each other to support and expand the Mōri clan."

Ichi-moji ni mitsu-boshi (kanji numeral one and three stars)

Takeda Shingen (1521–73)

Takeda Shingen had jurisdiction over the whole Shinano region. The battle of Kawanakajima, where Shingen fought against Uesugi Kenshin, is well known. Shingen was an excellent military strategist.

Wari-bishi or *Takeda-bishi* (divided rhombus)

Uesugi Kenshin (1530–78)

Kenshin, a general of the Echigo region, was another outstanding tactician. He went to Kyoto attempting to attack Oda Nobunaga, but died suddenly.

Take ni suzume or *Uesugi zasa* (sparrow and bamboo)

Shiba Tōshōgū shrine

Paper lantern at Shiba Tōshōgū shrine

Oda Nobunaga (1534–82)

Nobunaga, a general known for his daring and insolent personality, ruled Owari province and laid the groundwork for national unification.

Mokkō
Though his lineage was actually of the Inbe or Fujiwara clan, Nobunaga claimed that he was a descendant of Taira no Sukemori. Thus, he used the *mokkō* crest, which was well known as the crest of the Taira clan.

Toyotomi Hideyoshi (1536–98)

Originally from a peasant family in Owari, Hideyoshi was promoted to responsible positions by Oda Nobunaga, and eventually unified the country after his master's death.

Kiri (paulownia)
Hideyoshi seems to have had this crest granted to him by Nobunaga, when he had the surname Hashiba.

Tokugawa Ieyasu (1542–1616)

Ieyasu was the founder of the Tokugawa shogunate.

Mitsuba aoi (three hollyhock leaves, encircled)
The hollyhock originally belonged to the Matsudaira clan but, because of close family connections, it was also adopted by the Tokugawa clan.

Date Masamune (1567–1636)

Masamune was a one-eyed general known for his bravery. He fought for supremacy in the Tōhoku region.

Take ni suzume or *Sendai zasa* (sparrow and bamboo)

Map: Dominant Crests of the Edo Period

The crests depicted on this map are those of regionally powerful *daimyō* during the Edo period (1603–1867).

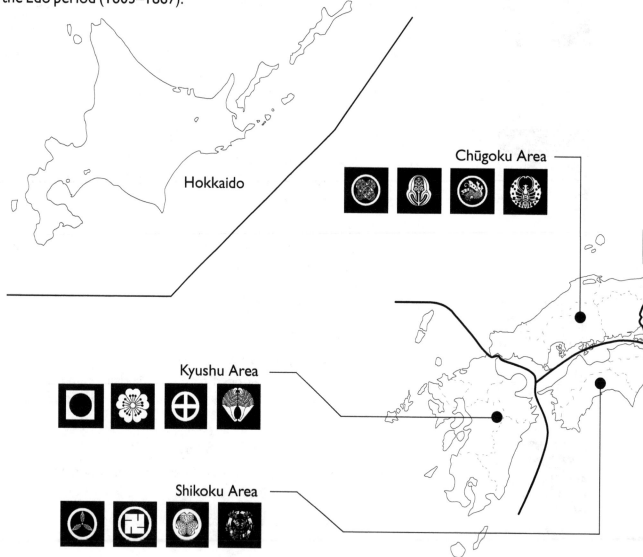

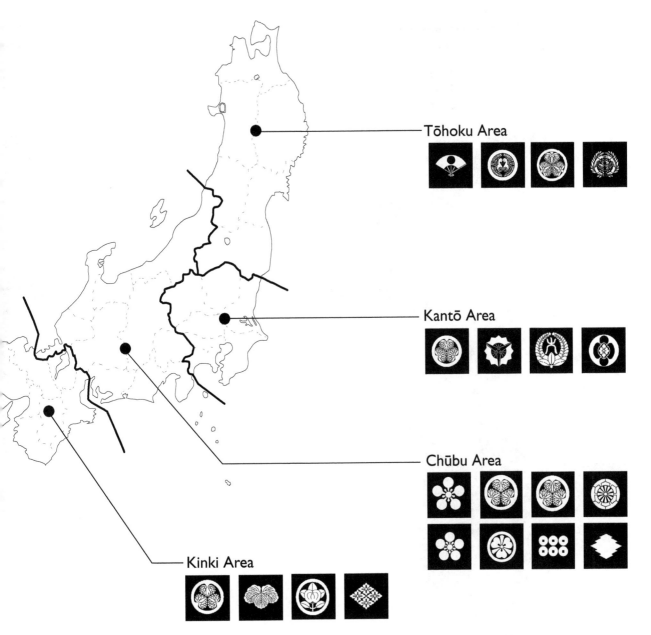

Tōhoku Area

Kantō Area

Chūbu Area

Kinki Area

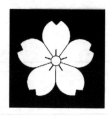

INDEX OF FAMILY CRESTS

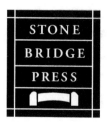

Other Titles of Interest from Stone Bridge Press

A Tractate on Japanese Aesthetics

DONALD RICHIE

In this new treatise on beauty in Japanese art, Richie looks at how perceptual values in Japan were drawn from raw nature and then modified by elegant expressions of class and taste. He explains aesthetic concepts like *wabi sabi, aware,* and *yugen,* and ponders their relevance in art and cinema today. Written in the manner of a *zuihitsu,* a free-ranging assortment of ideas that "follow the brush" wherever it leads.

80 pp, 5 x 7", paper, ISBN 978-1-933330-23-5, $9.95

Designing with Kanji

Japanese Character Motifs for Surface, Skin & Spirit

SHOGO OKETANI AND LEZA LOWITZ

Japanese *kanji* characters are full of meaning and beauty. But if you don't know the language, how do you find characters that say what you want and are not just a "kanji cliché"? This sampler has over 125 kanji in a fun format for easy use.

144 pp, 7 x 9", paper, 2-color printing throughout, 125 illustrations, ISBN 978-1-880656-79-2, $14.95

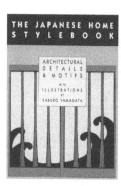

The Japanese Home Stylebook

Architectural Details and Motifs

ILLUSTRATIONS BY SABURO YAMAGATA; INTRODUCTION BY PETER GOODMAN

A definitive sourcebook for designers, architects, home remodelers, or anyone thinking of adding a Japan-inspired design to a room or home. Contains over 1,800 designs.

176 pp, 7 x 10", paper, ISBN 978-1-880656-01-3, $18.95

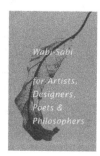

Wabi-Sabi

for Artists, Designers, Poets & Philosophers

LEONARD KOREN

A best-selling modern classic of design theory and ideals, this extended essay in words and pictures universalizes the Japanese traditional rustic aesthetic of *wabi-sabi*—the beauty of things imperfect, impermanent, and incomplete—that was developed over hundreds of years by priests and teamasters. "Perfectly conveys the Zen simplicity and stillness."—*Napra Review*

95 pp, 5½ x 8½", paper, 27 b/w photos, ISBN 978-1-880656-12-9, $14.95